Corridors of Time

Poetic Reflections on the Tapestry of Time

Peter I. Kattan

Petra Books

www.PetraBooks.com

Peter I. Kattan, PhD

Correspondence about this book may be sent to the author at one of the following two email addresses:

pkattan@petrabooks.com

info@petrabooks.com

Corridors of Time: Poetic Reflections on the Tapestry of Time

ISBN-13: 979-8-8691-8883-0

Preface

Welcome to "Corridors of Time: Poetic Reflections on the Tapestry of Time." This collection of poems explores the enigmatic essence of time and its profound impact on our lives, perceptions, and existence. Through verses woven with lyrical elegance and emotional depth, these poems endeavor to traverse the corridors of time, unraveling its mysteries and inviting contemplation on its multifaceted nature.

Time, that intangible force which governs the rhythm of our lives, has long captivated the human imagination. It is both a measure and a mystery, a constant companion and an elusive concept. In these verses, time is portrayed as a vast and intricate tapestry, interwoven with threads of memory, anticipation, and fleeting moments. Each poem serves as a thread in this tapestry, contributing to the rich and complex narrative of our temporal journey.

As we navigate through the corridors of time, we encounter moments of joy and sorrow, beginnings and endings, growth and decay. Through the poet's lens, time is not merely a linear progression but a kaleidoscope of experiences, emotions, and reflections. It is a river that flows inexorably onward, carrying us along its currents, shaping our destinies with its relentless momentum.

In this collection, the poets delve into the depths of time, contemplating its paradoxes and paradoxes. They explore the tension between the past, present, and future, the ephemeral nature of existence, and the eternal longing for meaning and immortality. Through their words, they invite readers to ponder the timeless questions that have intrigued philosophers and mystics throughout the ages: What is time? How do we perceive it? And what is our place within its vast expanse?

"Corridors of Time" is not merely a collection of poems but a journey of the soul, an exploration of the human experience in all its complexity and beauty. It is a testament to the power of poetry to transcend the boundaries of time and language, to touch the hearts and minds of readers across generations and cultures.

As you embark on this poetic journey, may these verses serve as companions and guides, illuminating the hidden recesses of the human spirit and inspiring contemplation on the nature of time and existence. May they remind us that, amidst the ceaseless passage of seconds and minutes, there are moments of beauty and transcendence that endure, forever etched in the corridors of time.

Most of the poems in this collection were generated using artificial intelligence. Specifically the latest version of ChatGPT (3.5) was used in this regard. There are 56 topics about time that are discussed with three poems presented for each topic. There is a total of 168 poems in this collection. The reader is encouraged to generate similar poems on their own. Note that the Exercises at the end of the book provide a comprehensive list of additional topics about time and the nature of time. It is recommended that the reader use these topics to generate more poems.

The author added about ten pages of original writing summarizing his speculations about time and the nature of time. These pages are shown at the beginning of this book and were written originally in

2002 but were never published before. It is the author's opinion that now after more than 20 years of their first revelation the time has come finally for these speculations to be made public.

With gratitude and reverence for the enduring mystery of time,

February 2024   Peter I. Kattan

Corridors of Time: Poetic Reflections on the Tapestry of Time

Contents

Corridors of Time: Poetic Reflections on the Tapestry of Time

Speculations

What is time? What is the relation between time and reality? Can time flow backwards? Is time travel possible? What is exactly the relationship between time and consciousness? Will there be an end to time? Is the speed of the passage of time uniform or variable? Is there a link between time and death? What is the relation between space and time? Can time flow be affected? What are coincidences and what is their relation to time? How many time dimensions are there? How is time measured? Is time discrete or continuous?

Time does not seem to flow with the same speed for all observers. Consider a human being, a baby and a cat. It does not seem that time flows in the same way for these three observers. It seems that a grown-up human being feels the passage of time differently than a baby or a cat. In fact, babies do not seem to notice the passage of time. Even cats and animals in general do not notice the passage of time. Most probably, the time dimension is not perceived by animals or even babies. With babies, their time dimension develops or grows with their growth. An hour or ten hours for a baby or a cat are almost the same interval. Obviously this is not the case for a grown-up human being. Obviously consciousness affects the passage of time. People usually think that time affects consciousness, but it is the other way around. Even for the same human being, time does not pass by in the same way at all times. When one is excited and enjoying himself or herself, time passes by quickly. However, when one is bored with nothing to do, time passes by slowly. It seems that with more information, time accelerates with increasing speed.

It is often said that time is the fourth dimension. This means that in addition to the three usual dimensions of space, we have one additional non-spatial dimension called time. However, before tackling the issue of the fourth dimension, we need to investigate the problem of the third dimension. Obviously, in space the three dimensions are identical. In space, one can move freely in any one of the three dimensions. However, on the planet Earth and on other planets, this does not seem to be the case. On Earth, one can move freely in two dimensions - east or west, north or south, but not up or down. The upward or downward motion is restricted by the force of gravity. Therefore, it seems that the third dimension (up or down) is linked to gravity. This shows that there is a relationship between gravity and dimensions. Since dimensions are also linked to time, we conclude that there is a relation between gravity and time.

Will there be an end to time? If we look at time these days and time about a million years ago, we conclude that it cannot be the same time. Before the advent of human beings, the passage of time could not have been measured in the same way we measure time these days. There was nobody present a million years ago to measure time or to even feel the passage of time. This means that a 100 years or a 1000 years are the same thing in the era of a million years ago. Thousands or millions of years could pass but there was no conscious observers to monitor them. This means that time as we know it today did not exist years ago. It is often said the beginning of time was the moment of the Big Bang. However, the beginning of time as we know it today was with the first grown-up conscious human being on Earth. Time could not have been observed or even have passed before that time.

We propose that the three space dimensions and time dimension evolved on this Earth since the moment of the Big Bang. We assume that the first space dimension appeared alone first. Them it was followed with the second space dimension then the third. Finally, the time dimension appeared only recently with the advent of human beings.

What is the exact relation between time and coincidences? In the normal flow of time (forward time), usually causes precede effects. When someone sees a tiger then thinks of a tiger, the cause is the seeing of the tiger and the effect is thinking about the tiger. However, when one thinks of a tiger then sees a tiger, this is called a coincidence or a synchronicity. In this regard, we have four cases. (1) Forward time flow with causes preceding effects. This is the usual case that happens every day. (2) Forward time flow with effects preceding   causes. These are the coincidences that happen. (3) Backward time flow with causes preceding effects. This case is identical to case 1. (4) Backward time flow with effects preceding causes. This case is identical to case 2.

The End of Time

What is the end of time? When will it occur? How will time end? What will happen exactly at the end of time? In this section, we make an attempt at answering these questions. The information presented in this section is partly based on the book "A New Model of the Universe" by Peter Ouspensky. We specifically used one idea in the chapter in the book entitled "A New Model of the Universe". However, most of the presentation is original by the author.

In the above chapter of Osupensky's book, he mentions that a point moving slowly along a straight line will appear as discrete points along the line. As the speed of motion of the point is increased, the point will move faster until it reaches a threshold speed after which there is no distinction between the discrete points. After this high speed limit, the motion of the point will become continuous and the motion will appear as a straight line. In this way, a new spatial dimension is created.

(Our motion through time is the like the point moving slowly along a straight line. It is clear that

we can move freely in the three dimensions of space but not in the time dimension. It is clear that the time dimension is different than the other three space dimensions. We cannot move freely in time. In this regard, time is an incomplete dimension of space. To complete the dimension of time, it will have to become a full space dimension at the end. This is what we mean by the end of time. As time progresses and moves faster, as we currently perceive it to do, we will reach a threshold limit after which will no longer be able to perceive time as discrete points as we do now. At that point, the time dimension will become a complete space dimension in which we can move freely. The current three dimensions of space will become four space dimensions. This is exactly what will happen at the end of time. Time will no longer be. It will replaced by a fourth dimension of space.

In the transformation from three dimensions of space to four space dimensions, it is anticipated that the human body will also transform. Either a radical transformation will occur or we will at least develop some new organs to use them to see the new dimension and move freely in it. However, how this transformation will occur is not yet clear. It may happen in two different ways: (1) the fourth space dimension will emerge smoothly and complement the three existing space dimensions, or (2) the current three space dimensions will collapse or change and four new space dimensions will emerge. Whatever way it happens, the transformation is expected to be sudden. It will happen suddenly at the moment of the end of time or what is called the Omega Point. It is widely anticipated that this will occur in or around the year 2012. We are currently experiencing some sort of speeding of time and all indications point to a radical transformation that will occur soon. It is anticipated that this will be accompanied by the emergence of a new species.

Today in 2024, the year 2012 passed with no events whatsoever. Thus the passages above and below about the year 2012 should be considered to apply to a future year. The arguments presented are still valid but the time and year specified is wrong. This should be taken into account when reading these speculations.)

As we approach 2012, an exponential increase in the amount of information will occur. The information in one hour in 2012 will be comparable to the information in one year in the 1980s. Furthermore, all rigid systems will collapse as we approach 2012 including political, religious, social and economic systems. This is because rigid systems will not be able to withstand the changes that will occur as we approach 2012. They will all be replaced by one global flexible system as the Omega Point approaches. The sole purpose of this new system is to bring in the new space dimension. This new system will be favorably suited to withstand all the changes that will occur as the Omega Point approaches.

It should be mentioned that the events that will transpire as 2012 approaches are so shocking emotionally to the planet consciousness that these events have sent foreshocks reverberating in the past. Many of the events that will occur have been seen by certain psychics and prophets of old. The reader should look in the prophetic literature to have a clue of what will transpire as the end of time approaches.

Information and Health

A system that has more information content is more healthy. This is attributed to the fact that a system that has more information content is more complex in nature. Applying this to a human body, it is seen that a human body with more information content that is complex will be healthier than another human body with less information. The complexity of the human body increases its health attributes. Consequently, a person may be able to raise his immunity and increase his health by increasing the amount of information that he has.

There are many methods in which one can increase his or her information content. Methods such as reading books, browsing the internet, listening to music, etc are all meant to increase the information content of the person. However, there are indications that these methods are affected by the mood of the person while acquiring information. An energetic and enthusiastic mood will help to attract more information than a bored and gloomy mood. So when using these methods, make sure there is an atmosphere of excitement and enjoyment around you or inside you.

Events and Time:

It is well known that events affect both space and time. An event affects the space surrounding it and the time period following its occurrence. But can an event affect the time period preceding its occurrence? This is what we will attempt to answer in this section.

When an event occurs it affects the space around its point of occurrence. Suppose the event is an explosion of some sort. If the event is uniform, then its spatial effect will be circular in geometry. However, if the event is not uniform, then its spatial effect will be an arbitrary shape. Most events are not uniform.

When an event like an explosion occurs, in addition to affecting the spatial area surrounding it, it also affects the time period following its occurrence. In certain types of events which are very emotional or shocking or horrible, the time period preceding its occurrence is affected to a certain degree. In this case, the event sends signals or detectable effects back to the past. These signals may take the form of accidents, synchronicities, telepathic messages, increased earthquake activity, etc. These signals can be detected and calculated in order to devise a strategy to predict the horrible event.

Anti-time:

We will look now briefly at the concept of anti-time. This is a theoretical concept of a time component emerging that is essentially the reverse of the normal flow of the time dimension. Anti-time may be regarded as time flowing backwards - opposite normal time. It is anticipated that if time and anti-time meet (or collide), certain disruption is space will occur. This event is expected to occur towards the period of the end of time. Toward the end of time, an anti-time component will emerge and collide with normal time. The effects of such a collision will be large disruptions in the space-time continuum in the form of astronomical and geophysical disturbances. The astronomical ones will be in the form of gamma ray bursts and solar disruption and the geophysical ones will be in the form of earthquakes and volcanos. The final outcome of such an event is the annihilation of both time and anti-time and the emergence of the new space dimension.

Health and Extension over Time:

I will talk now about my concept of extension over time and its relation to the health of the human body. According to the latest theories of physics (i.e. Einstein's theory of relativity), time does not flow from the past to the present to the future. The past, the present, and the future exist simultaneously. It is even claimed that the both the past and the future can be accessed. After all, some sort of time travel may be possible. If the past and the future are available now, then you can extend yourself over time. By "yourself", I mean your body and/or consciousness. This extension may be done using several methods like praying and visualization. You can pray for past events and future events. You can visualize past events and future events. If these methods are maintained on a regular basis, then you will be extending yourself over time. In effect, you become four-dimensional.

Now, how is this extension over time related to health? When you become four-dimensional and think in a four dimensional way, you decrease your existence in the physical three- dimensional world. In addition, your immunity system will be tremendously boosted, i.e your immunity will be greatly increased. Thus you will be less likely to be attacked by viruses and bacteria which are three-dimensional or in some cases even two-dimensional. In effect, you become invisible to the germs. Thus we see that extension over time will keep your body healthy and vibrant. If this method is coupled with the method of increasing the information content of the body/consciousness, then together these two methods will be effective tools in increasing your immunity and keeping the body healthy.

Changing the Past:

Can the past be changed? Can we change the past? Has the past been changed? These are questions that we need to answer? If the past has been changed, how would we know of the change? If the past has been changed, then our memories would have changed also. Suppose that an old past was somehow changed into a new past. Then our memories of the old past were also changed into memories of the new past. We would not now know of the old past because those memories were lost. Therefore, if the past has been changed, we have currently no way of knowing it, especially with the current capabilities of the human brain. To know of the change of the past, a human being must retain two sets of memories - memories of the old past and memories of the new past. Therefore, a human being must be able to work across timelines.

Timelines are different world histories or worlds according to one interpretation of quantum mechanics. Unless this ability of being aware across multiple timelines is manifested, we would never know of any change made to the past.

Recommended Books to Read: (Check the references at the end of the book)

1. Time Storms
2. Timewarps
3. Time

Theories of Time:

1. Einstein's theory of relativity - spacetime
2. Dune's theory of serial time.
3. Priestley's theories in his book "Man and Time"
4. Gribbin in his book "Timewarps"
5. Ouspensky's three dimensions of time
6. Kozyrev's properties of time
7. Symelov's golden ratio and sequence of time
8. Timewave zero fractals and Terence McKenna
9. Colin Wilson's thoughts in his books on supernatural phenomena
10. McMoneagle's time theory using the mind with his remote viewing experiments
11. Eternal recurrence of Osupensky
12. Three times of time of Montalk - Time to protect
13. Time according to quantum mechanics
14. Time according to astronomy - sidereal time, etc
15. Multiverse theory of time according to David Deutsch

"Time" Songs:

1. Time, Tears for Fears
2. Time after time, Cyndi Loper
3. Hold me now, Johnny Logan

Time. We cannot see it. We cannot hear it. We cannot smell it. We cannot taste it. We cannot touch it. How then can we perceive it? Does it exist? We cannot perceive it with the five senses yet we know about it. We feel its passage continuously. How do we then know that time passes? May be with the mind!! Is time a phenomenon of mind or consciousness?

The Nature of Time -1-

In the silent sweep of time's embrace,
A dance of moments, each a trace,
Of dreams unfurling, in its flight,
A tapestry woven of day and night.

It whispers secrets in the dawn,
And paints the sky as day is born.
With gentle touch, it guides the stream,
Of life's unfolding, like a dream.

Through seasons' turn, it takes its toll,
As memories bloom and stories unfold.
It's both a friend and a foe, they say,
A fleeting wisp, yet here to stay.

In every heartbeat, it leaves its mark,
A journey carved through light and dark.
It bends and twists, with no refrain,
A constant flux, yet bound by chain.

It's measured in seconds, counted in years,
Yet holds the weight of joys and fears.
It slips away, yet leaves its trace,
In every smile and furrowed face.

Oh, elusive time, forever in flight,
A puzzle unsolved, a guiding light.
In its passage, we find our rhyme,
A fleeting glimpse of the grand design.

The Nature of Time -2-

In the boundless expanse where moments weave,
Time dances silently, yet we perceive.
A river flowing, ceaseless and vast,
From future dreams to the distant past.

It wraps around us like a shroud,
Whispering secrets, soft yet loud.
Eternal paradox, fleeting and still,
It bends our will to its silent thrill.

In the morning's light, it gently wakes,
With each heartbeat, a journey it makes.
Through sunlit meadows and starlit skies,
It paints its canvas with silent sighs.

It marks the seasons with its subtle hand,
Turning the pages of life's grand stand.
From youth's tender bloom to age's wane,
It writes its story, a timeless refrain.

Yet in its passage, we find our grace,
Embracing each moment, a sacred space.
For in the tapestry of time we find,
The essence of life, intertwined.

So let us cherish each fleeting hour,
For time's embrace holds endless power.
In its rhythm, we find our rhyme,
A symphony echoing through the sands of time.

The Nature of Time -3-

In the realm where seconds softly flee,
Time's enigma whispers to you and me.
A silent witness to life's grand design,
It bends and weaves, a mastermind divine.

With every sunrise, a new chapter unfolds,
In time's embrace, our story molds.
Through laughter and tears, it guides our way,
A silent companion, night and day.

It's the measure of moments, the keeper of dreams,
A river flowing through life's endless streams.
It teaches us patience, in its steady flow,
And reminds us that nothing truly does grow.

In its boundless expanse, we find our place,
A speck in the cosmic race.
Yet within its grasp, we hold the key,
To unlock the mysteries of eternity.

So let us honor each tick and tock,
As time's gentle hands wind the clock.
For in its passage, we find our truth,
In the fleeting moments of our youth.

Time Travel -1-

In the tapestry of time, a traveler's quest
A journey through ages, the very best.
Through cosmic threads, a portal unfolds,
Whispers of futures and tales of old.

Through the warp and weft of temporal streams,
A dance with destiny, beyond our dreams.
Chronicles unfurl in a mystical rhyme,
A symphony of epochs, a dance through time.

In a vessel of light, through the celestial gate,
A pilgrim embarks on a voyage so great.
Past echoes whisper, futures beckon near,
Temporal winds guide, allaying the fear.

A clockwork continuum, ticking away,
Moments entwined in a cosmic ballet.
The past, a canvas of yesterdays' grace,
The future, a mystery, awaiting embrace.

Through eras untold, where empires rise,
And civilizations fall, under changing skies.
The traveler witnesses the ebb and flow,
Of history's river, where echoes grow.

Through the corridors of time, the wanderer strides,
Where paradoxes dance, and reality hides.
The hands of the clock, an unwavering guide,
As the traveler navigates the temporal tide.

Yet, caution be taken in this wondrous flight,
For meddling with time may alter the light.
A delicate balance, a precarious line,
Where destinies shift, and realities entwine.

In the tapestry of time, the journey's end,
A return to the present, a message to send.
For every moment, a chapter to scribe,
In the grand book of time, where futures thrive.

Time Travel -2-

Beneath the starry quilt of the cosmic sea,
A time traveler sails, unbound and free.
Through corridors unseen, where seconds weave,
The fabric of ages, in which stories cleave.

A vessel of dreams, through epochs untold,
In the grasp of time's fingers, both young and old.
A chrononaut's journey, through the ethereal stream,
A dance with destiny, a cosmic, timeless dream.

Past and future entwine in a waltz so divine,
Moments as whispers, in the celestial design.
The traveler gazes upon the tapestry vast,
A kaleidoscope of memories, present, and past.

On the threshold of eras, in the time-traveler's wake,
Chronicles unfold, every decision they make.
Through ancient ruins and futures unknown,
A symphony of time in a harmonic tone.

In the realm of paradox, where realities sway,
The traveler navigates, a beacon in the astral array.
Each leap into the unknown, a courageous flight,
As the past and the future embrace the traveler's light.

A dance with anomalies, a ballet with fate,
Through the fabric of time, the explorer creates.
In the tapestry's loom, where destinies twine,
The time traveler weaves, a narrative divine.

Yet heed the caution, in the chronicles spun,
For time is a master, and its dance must be done.
A cosmic ballet, where past, present, and morrow,
Interlace in a dance, a continuum to borrow.

Time Travel -3-

Beneath the cloak of celestial stardust spun,
A time traveler journeys, with the setting sun.
Through the ebb and flow of the temporal tide,
They embark on a quest, where worlds coincide.

In the corridors of ages, a cosmic ballet,
Footprints left in the sands of yesterday.
A vessel of wonder through the quantum sea,
A navigator of time, wild and free.

The hands of the clock, a silent guide,
As the traveler transcends, with time as their guide.
Past and future entangled, a dance sublime,
A journey through echoes, a poet's rhyme.

The past, a canvas of sepia-toned lore,
Where ancient whispers linger, forevermore.
The future, a canvas yet to be unfurled,
An unwritten tale in the fabric of the world.

Through the veil of years, the traveler strides,
In the river of time, where destiny hides.
Each moment a gem, both precious and rare,
A symphony of moments, suspended in air.

Yet caution prevails in this temporal waltz,
For the dance with time holds unforeseen faults.
As the traveler glimpses both what was and will be,
They leave imprints on time, like ripples in the sea.

So sail, O traveler, through the cosmic expanse,
With courage and wonder, take destiny's chance.
In the grandeur of time, let your story unfurl,
A chronicle written in the eternal swirl.

Time and Changing the Past -1-

In the ceaseless flow of time's relentless tide,
We ponder moments where we might confide,
Yearning to grasp what slips through our hand,
The past, a canvas we cannot command.

In the hush of night, when memories dance,
We dwell on chances, on a fleeting glance,
For time, the sculptor of destiny's cast,
Remains indifferent to wishes amassed.

Yet whispers linger of a mystical art,
To rewind the clocks, to restart,
To mend the fractures in history's seam,
And rewrite the tales of what might have been.

Oh, how we dream of altering fate's decree,
Erasing missteps, setting our hearts free,
But time, a master with rules unbent,
Mocks our desires, leaving us discontent.

For each alteration, a ripple unfurls,
Affecting the tapestry of the world,
And though we crave to rectify our past,
It's in the present where our journey's cast.

So let us cherish the moments we hold,
For time's embrace is both fierce and bold,
And while we cannot rewrite what's gone by,
We can shape the future beneath the sky.

With every breath, with each step we take,
We mold our destiny, for love's sake,
Embracing change, with courage amassed,
For time, the eternal, is ours to grasp.

Time and Changing the Past -2-

In the sands of time, where echoes softly sigh,
Whispers of yesterday flutter and fly,
A longing to grasp what once slipped away,
To rewind the clock, to a bygone day.

In the labyrinth of memories, we roam,
Seeking solace in the forgotten tome,
Yearning to alter the course of the past,
To erase the shadows that forever last.

But time, the guardian of all that's been,
Holds fast to the secrets it has seen,
With each tick of the clock, it gently reminds,
The past is a ghost, forever confined.

Yet within the heart, a flame still burns bright,
A beacon of hope in the depths of night,
For though we cannot change what has been done,
We can forge a new path, with each rising sun.

So let us embrace the gift of today,
And weave our dreams in the light's gentle sway,
For time may be fleeting, but love is the key,
To unlock the future, and set our spirits free.

Time and Changing the Past -3-

In the realm where time's fingers softly weave,
Memories flicker, in shadows they cleave.
Whispers of moments, once lived and known,
Echo through chambers, where dreams are sown.

Yearning to grasp what's slipped from our hold,
To rewrite the tale, to change what's been told.
In the quiet depths where regrets do reside,
We seek solace in the waves of time's tide.

Yet time, like a river, flows ever on,
Carrying with it the deeds that are gone.
Though we may yearn for a chance to amend,
The past remains steadfast, its lessons to send.

But in this present, where our footsteps tread,
Lies the power to shape what lies ahead.
With courage and grace, we face the unknown,
Embracing the journey, together we've sewn.

So let us not dwell on what's left behind,
For in the passage of time, new treasures we find.
With hope as our compass, we chart our own way,
In the ever-changing dance of night and day.

Time and the Future -1-

In the tapestry of time, we weave,
Threads of past, present, future cleave.
Through the vast expanse, we roam,
Seeking secrets yet unknown.

In the dawn of tomorrow's light,
We glimpse the future, shining bright.
A realm of dreams, of hopes untold,
Where destinies and fates unfold.

The clock's hands tick, relentless, sure,
Marking moments, swift and pure.
Each second whispers tales anew,
Of paths diverging, skies of blue.

Yet time, the master, ever wields,
Its power vast, its mystery shields.
For in its grasp, we're but a mote,
A fleeting breath, a whispered note.

But fear not the unknown ahead,
For time is but a riverbed.
Flowing onward, ever true,
Guiding us to all we'll do.

So let us greet the future's call,
Embrace its wonders, stand tall.
For in the dance of time's embrace,
We find our purpose, our rightful place.

Time and the Future -2-

In the tapestry of eternity's rhyme,
We glimpse the future, a distant chime.
Time's canvas vast, stretched wide and far,
Holding secrets, like a guiding star.

Through the mist of moments yet to be,
We wander, curious, wild and free.
The future's promise, a beacon bright,
Illuminating the darkest night.

In the cradle of tomorrow's dawn,
We plant the seeds of dreams, reborn.
Each choice we make, each step we take,
Shapes the destiny we'll partake.

But time, oh time, an enigma profound,
Its depths unfathomed, its mysteries unbound.
We journey forward, with hearts ablaze,
Navigating the maze of future days.

So let us embrace the unknown ahead,
With courage, with faith, by hope we're led.
For in the tapestry of time's embrace,
We find the beauty of life's endless grace.

Time and the Future -3-

In the realm where dreams and futures blend,
Time's endless river, its course to mend.
We sail upon its flowing stream,
Chasing visions, lost in the gleam.

The future calls, a siren's song,
Beckoning us where we belong.
With every heartbeat, every sigh,
We journey forth, beneath the sky.

In the silence of the coming years,
We confront our hopes, our deepest fears.
But in the unknown, there lies the key,
To unlock the treasures yet to be.

For time is but a gentle guide,
Leading us to where fate may bide.
With every moment, every choice,
We find our voice, we raise our voice.

So let us dance upon the stage,
Of life's grand play, from age to age.
Embrace the future, bold and bright,
And paint the canvas with love's pure light.

Time and the Present Moment -1-

In the realm where time dances, ever grand,
There lies a moment, precious, in our hand.
It's now, the present, where life's stories blend,
A fleeting whisper, on which all moments depend.

Time, a river ceaselessly flowing,
Through valleys of memory, constantly glowing.
Yet in the present, it finds its grace,
A sacred space where all moments embrace.

Each second a gift, a treasure untold,
In the tapestry of time, its threads unfold.
The past, a shadow, the future, a dream,
But the present, a jewel in life's vast scheme.

In its grasp, we find the power to be,
To shape our destiny, to set our souls free.
For in this moment, all is reborn,
The past forgiven, the future adorned.

Let us cherish the now, this moment divine,
For in its embrace, true joy we find.
Time may march on with relentless stride,
But the present moment, it's here to abide.

So let us live fully, with hearts open wide,
In the eternal dance of time, let us reside.
For in the now, we find our truest self,
In the timeless embrace of life itself.

Time and the Present Moment -2-

In the hush of twilight's soft embrace,
Where time and space interlace,
There lies a moment, pure and still,
Where dreams take flight, and hearts fulfill.

It's in this space, this sacred zone,
Where past and future melt and hone.
The present moment, ever bright,
A beacon in the darkest night.

Through shifting sands of fleeting time,
It stands as steadfast as a chime.
A melody that softly sings,
Of life's unfolding, with all its wings.

In this moment, we find our power,
To bloom like flowers after a shower.
To seize the day, to seize the hour,
And bask in life's most precious dower.

Let not the past confine our sight,
Nor future's worries dim the light.
For in the now, we hold the key,
To shape our fate, to truly be.

So let us dance in this expanse,
Where time's illusion takes its stance.
For in the present, we are whole,
A symphony of heart and soul.

Time and the Present Moment -3-

In the quiet whispers of dawn's first light,
Where shadows fade and dreams take flight,
There lies a moment, pristine and clear,
Where time stands still, and all is near.

It's in this space, this gentle pause,
Where life's mysteries unfold like gauze.
The present moment, a sacred gift,
A chance to heal, to soar, to uplift.

Through the ebb and flow of days gone by,
The present moment is where we lie.
An anchor in the vast expanse,
A fleeting glance, a cosmic dance.

In this moment, we find our grace,
A chance to rise, to find our place.
To savor each breath, each beat of heart,
And let the universe play its part.

Let not regrets of yesterday,
Nor fears of tomorrow lead astray.
For in the now, we find our truth,
Infinite potential, eternal youth.

So let us embrace this fleeting time,
With open arms, with soulful rhyme.
For in the present, we are free,
To write our own reality.

Time and Memory -1-

In the realm where time entwines with memory's
grace,
A dance of moments, an eternal embrace.
Through the corridors of our minds, it weaves,
The tapestry of our lives, where each memory
cleaves.

In the hushed whispers of the ticking clock,
Echoes the past, in each tick and tock.
Time, the river, ceaselessly flows,
Carrying memories wherever it goes.

In the amber glow of twilight's gleam,
We drift along, in a nostalgic dream.
Recalling laughter, tears, and sighs,
As time's gentle touch upon us lies.

Memories like stars, they twinkle and fade,
Yet in the heart's recesses, they're forever laid.
They paint the canvas of our soul's expanse,
Each one a story, a fleeting chance.

Time, the sculptor, molds our yesterdays,
Etching them in the labyrinthine maze.
Each moment lived, each memory dear,
In the grand symphony of life, they appear.

So let us cherish the moments we find,
For time's swift passage leaves no one behind.
And in the treasury of memory's keep,
Our timeless stories eternally sleep.

Time and Memory -2-

In the garden of memory, time's flowers bloom,
Each petal a moment, dispelling gloom.
They sway in the breeze of days gone by,
Whispering secrets, reaching for the sky.

Through the corridors of time, we wander,
Lost in the echoes of joy and wonder.
Fragments of laughter, fragments of pain,
Bound together in memory's chain.

The hands of the clock spin tales untold,
Of love that blossomed, of dreams that unfold.
In the tapestry of life, each thread weaves,
A story of hopes, of losses, of leaves.

But time is a river, ever flowing,
Its currents relentless, always growing.
Memories drift like autumn leaves,
In the gentle sway of time's reprieves.

So let us savor each moment we're given,
For in memory's embrace, we are driven.
To cherish the past, embrace the now,
For time and memory, hand in hand, we avow.

Time and Memory -3-

In the caverns of time, where memories dwell,
Echoes of moments, a whispered spell.
Time's steady march, relentless and sure,
Leaves imprints of stories, both vivid and pure.

In the vaults of remembrance, shadows dance,
Capturing fragments of life's fleeting chance.
Each memory a jewel, both precious and rare,
A mosaic of emotions, laid bare.

Through the corridors of our mind's domain,
We journey, seeking solace from the pain.
In the recesses of memory's embrace,
We find comfort, a sacred space.

Yet time, the relentless tide, does not relent,
It carries us forward, wherever we're sent.
But in the tapestry of time's grand design,
Our memories shimmer, eternally divine.

So let us treasure each moment we hold dear,
For time's passage is swift, its end unclear.
In the symphony of life, let memories chime,
For in their embrace, we transcend time.

Time and Mind -1-

In the dance of moments, time does unwind,
A tapestry woven within the mind.
It flows like a river, swift and serene,
Through valleys of memory, a constant scene.

In the depths of thought, it finds its sway,
Guiding our steps through night and day.
Tick-tock, the clock beats its refrain,
As seconds slip by, a fleeting chain.

The past, a shadow, cast upon the wall,
A whisper of echoes, a distant call.
The future, a dream, yet to unfold,
A canvas of possibilities, bold and untold.

But in the present, where moments reside,
The heart finds solace, the soul's true guide.
For time is a gift, both precious and rare,
To cherish and embrace, with love and care.

So let us embrace each passing hour,
With gratitude, humility, and power.
For in the union of time and mind,
Lies the beauty of life, intertwined.

Time and Mind -2-

In the labyrinth of thought, where time does roam,
The mind becomes a palace, a sacred home.
Through corridors of memory, it wanders free,
Exploring the depths of its own mystery.

Each tick of the clock, a heartbeat's sound,
Echoing through the chambers profound.
In the tapestry of dreams, it weaves its tale,
A symphony of whispers, a celestial sail.

The past, a constellation in the night,
A map of where we've been, our guiding light.
The future, a horizon yet to be,
A canvas of possibilities, vast and free.

But in the silence of the present's embrace,
The mind finds stillness, a sacred space.
Here, time loses its grip, its hold,
As we surrender to the moment, bold.

For in the union of time and mind's embrace,
We find the essence of our human grace.
In each fleeting moment, we're alive,
Infinite possibilities, waiting to thrive.

So let us honor this dance, this divine rhyme,
In the eternal union of time and mind.

Time and Mind -3-

In the realm where time and mind entwine,
A symphony of moments, divine.
Time, a river flowing ceaselessly,
Mind, a vessel sailing endlessly.

Through the corridors of memory's keep,
Whispers of yesterday softly creep.
Echoes of laughter, tears, and sighs,
In the chambers of the mind, they rise.

But time is more than just a stream,
It's a beacon lighting up our dream.
In the tapestry of our deepest thought,
It weaves the stories we've sought.

Each passing second, a precious gem,
In the crown of life's diadem.
For in the present, where moments reside,
The true essence of existence abides.

So let us navigate this boundless sea,
With the compass of our humanity.
In the union of time and mind's embrace,
We find our purpose, our sacred place.

Time and Consciousness -1-

In the flow of time, our consciousness roams,
A voyage through realms, where moments compose.
From dawn's first light to twilight's gentle hue,
We dance with time, embracing what is true.

Each tick of the clock, a heartbeat's refrain,
Echoes of existence, joy, and pain.
In the tapestry of life, we find our place,
Weaving through time with dignity and grace.

Through the corridors of memory, we roam,
In the labyrinth of time, finding our home.
The past, a whisper, the future, a dream,
In the present moment, life's secrets gleam.

With every passing second, we evolve,
Time's ceaseless march, our problems resolve.
Yet, in its rhythm, a melody we find,
A symphony of moments, intertwined.

Time, the sculptor of our destinies,
Shaping our consciousness with its mysteries.
In its embrace, we ponder and we grow,
Navigating life's currents, ebb, and flow.

So let us savor each fleeting hour,
Embrace the beauty, the depth, the power.
For in the dance of time and consciousness,
We find the essence of our existence's finesse.

Time and Consciousness -2-

In the depths of time, where consciousness resides,
A journey unfolds, where souls take their strides.
With every beat of the heart, a rhythm plays,
In the dance of existence, where time sways.

Through the corridors of the mind, we roam,
Exploring the vastness of our inner home.
Memories flicker like stars in the night,
Guiding us through darkness, towards the light.

Time, a river flowing endlessly,
Carrying us along, towards our destiny.
In its currents, we find our place,
Navigating the waters with courage and grace.

Consciousness, a flame burning bright,
Illuminating the darkness of the night.
With every thought, a universe is born,
In the infinite expanse, we are reborn.

So let us cherish each moment we find,
In the tapestry of time, intertwined.
For in the union of consciousness and time,
We discover the essence of the sublime.

Time and Consciousness -3-

In the timeless realm where consciousness reigns,
A symphony of thoughts, emotions, and pains.
Through the vast expanse of the mind,
we soar, Exploring the depths, seeking evermore.

Time, the silent witness to our plight,
A constant companion in the day and night.
Its steady march shapes our reality,
Guiding us through life's intricate tapestry.

Each moment a brushstroke upon the canvas of fate,
Weaving together love, loss, and debate.
In the grand theater of existence, we play our part,
Bound by the threads of time, connected at heart.

Consciousness, the beacon that lights our way,
Leading us through the shadows, come what may.
In its depths, we find our truest selves,
Reflecting the essence of all that delves.

So let us embrace the dance of time and mind,
In its ebb and flow, wisdom we find.
For in the nexus of consciousness and time's
embrace,
Lies the secret to life's eternal grace.

Time and Reality -1-

In the realm where time and reality dance,
Moments flicker like flames in a trance.
Through the corridors of eternity's hall,
We wander, ever heeding its call.

Time, the weaver of stories untold,
In its tapestry, destinies unfold.
Yet reality, elusive and strange,
Shifts and shimmers, inconstant in range.

Like rivers that flow and mountains that rise,
Time's passage, a truth that never dies.
In the quiet whispers of the night,
Reality wavers, casting its light.

Each tick of the clock, a beat of the heart,
Binding us to this world, never to depart.
Yet in dreams, we escape its hold,
Exploring realms where mysteries unfold.

Oh, how time and reality intertwine,
In the fabric of existence, they define.
Moments fleeting, yet eternally true,
In the dance of life, we find our due.

So let us embrace each passing hour,
In the tapestry of time, find our power.
For in the union of reality's grace,
We discover the beauty of life's embrace.

Time and Reality -2-

In the vast expanse where time unfurls,
Reality's cloak wraps 'round the world.
Time, the silent marcher, never still,
Reality, a canvas we bend to our will.

Through the corridors of history's gaze,
Time's steady rhythm sets the stage.
Each second a verse, each minute a rhyme,
Weaving tales of splendor, marking the climb.

Reality, a mirror reflecting our truth,
Reveals the essence of age and youth.
In its depths, we find the echoes of dreams,
And the whispers of hope in silent streams.

Time, relentless in its steady stride,
Carves memories deep, where shadows hide.
Yet reality's brush, with colors bright,
Paints visions of dawn in the darkest night.

Together they dance, in cosmic embrace,
Shaping our journey, leaving no trace.
In the symphony of existence, they entwine,
Guiding our steps through the sands of time.

So let us savor each moment's grace,
Embrace the present, in its fleeting pace.
For in the tapestry of time and reality's hue,
We find the beauty of life, forever anew.

Time and Reality -3-

In the tapestry of time, we're woven tight,
Threads of existence, in the dark and light.
Reality's canvas, ever shifting and vast,
Holds the stories of future, present, and past.

Time, the sculptor of moments, relentless and bold,
Carves out our journey, in silver and gold.
Each tick of the clock, a whisper of fate,
Guiding our steps, before it's too late.

Reality, the mirror reflecting our soul,
Shows the fragments of who we are, as a whole.
In its reflection, we see our dreams take flight,
And the shadows that dance in the depths of night.

Together they merge, in a dance divine,
Crafting the narrative of life's design.
In the interplay of time and reality's song,
We find our purpose, where we belong.

So cherish each second, each breath that you take,
For time's fleeting passage, no one can forsake.
In the embrace of reality's gentle sway,
We find the magic of each passing day.

Time and the Brain -1-

In the caverns of the mind, where neurons fire and
dance,
Time weaves its silent threads, in an intricate trance.
A tapestry of memories, a mosaic of thought,
In the labyrinth of the brain, time is both sought.

Tick-tock, the clock chimes, in the corridors of the
mind,
Moments frozen in amber, yet slipping behind.
For time is but a phantom, a specter of the soul,
In the depths of consciousness, its mysteries unfold.

In dreams, it stretches endlessly, a boundless
expanse,
But in waking hours, it quickens, caught in life's
dance.
Each heartbeat, each breath, a rhythm of its own,
Yet time's passage remains an enigma, unknown.

Memories flicker like candlelight, casting shadows on
the wall,
Moments etched in neurons, waiting for time's call.
For the brain is a vessel, where time's currents flow,
Navigating the waters of past, present, and tomorrow.

Through the corridors of thought, time's echoes softly
hum,
A symphony of existence, where past and present
become one.
In the tapestry of the mind, where neurons intertwine,
Time's melody plays on, an eternal design.

So let us cherish each moment, as time slips away,
For in the recesses of the brain, it forever holds sway.
In the dance of neurons, in the depths of the mind,
Time's essence lingers, an eternal bind.

Time and the Brain -2-

In the quiet chambers of the brain, time whispers its
tale,
A silent symphony, a winding trail.
Neurons spark and synapses blaze,
As time's rhythm guides the mind's maze.

In the dance of thought, in the depths of the mind,
Time weaves its threads, intricate and kind.
Memories bloom like flowers in spring,
Each moment a melody, each memory a wing.

Tick-tock, the clock echoes, steady and sure,
As time's currents flow, relentless and pure.
Yet in the mind's sanctuary, time finds its rest,
In the embrace of consciousness, it's endlessly
blessed.

For time is a river, winding and free,
Carrying the soul on its journey, through eternity.
In the tapestry of the brain, it paints its scenes,
A canvas of existence, woven in dreams.

So let us ponder the mysteries, the wonders untold,
In the vast expanse of the mind, where time unfolds.
For in the labyrinth of thought, in the depths of the
brain,
Time's eternal presence, forever shall reign.

Time and the Brain -3-

In the chambers of the mind, where thoughts take
flight,
Time dances softly, in shadows of light.
Neurons spark and synapses bloom,
In the ever-turning wheel of time's silent loom.

Memories like whispers, echo and fade,
In the tapestry of the brain, where dreams are made.
Each moment a ripple, in the river of thought,
As time's gentle current carries what's sought.
T
ick-tock, the clock sings its ancient song,
In the symphony of existence, where we all belong.
Yet in the recesses of the mind, time finds its sway,
A kaleidoscope of moments, in the theater of the day.

For time is a sculptor, shaping our minds,
Etching its mark on the fabric of time.
In the depths of consciousness, it weaves its spell,
A timeless dance, where all things dwell.

So let us embrace the mystery, the wonder untold,
In the enigma of time, where stories unfold.
For in the labyrinth of the brain, where dreams are
spun,
Time and the mind are forever one.

Psychological Time -1-

In the realm where seconds stretch and bend,
Lies the psyche's vast expanse, a maze to wend.
Time, not just a ticking clock on the wall,
But a labyrinth of the mind, where shadows fall.

It's not the steady march of hours that we chase,
But the ebb and flow of memories, leaving their trace.
Moments elongate, suspended in air,
Or race by like shooting stars, swift and rare.

In the depths of thought, where dreams take flight,
Psychological time dances in the dimming light.
It's the heartbeat of anticipation, the sigh of regret,
A tapestry of emotions, tangled and set.

Yesterday's regrets and tomorrow's fears,
Conspire in the mind, shedding silent tears.
They warp perception, distort the view,
Rendering the present a hazy hue.

Yet in this tangled web of past and future's grasp,
There lies the beauty, the moments we clasp.
For within the chaos, there's a rhythm, a rhyme,
A melody of the soul, in psychological time.

So let us not be slaves to the ticking of the clock,
But embrace the dance, let our spirits unlock.
For in the dance of the mind, we find our true grace,
And in each fleeting moment, a sacred space.

Psychological Time -2-

In the depths of the mind, where mysteries unfold,
Lies a realm untouched by clocks, a story yet untold.
Psychological time, a river winding through the soul,
Carries memories and dreams, making us whole.

It's not the ticking of hands that guides our way,
But the echoes of laughter and the shadows of
dismay.
Each moment a painting, vivid and alive,
As we navigate the currents, striving to survive.

In the caverns of thought, where echoes softly speak,
Psychological time flows, both strong and meek.
It's the whisper of desires and the echoes of pain,
A journey through the psyche, where nothing remains
the same.

Past, present, future, intertwined in the dance,
As we grapple with existence, taking every chance.
For time is not linear, but a circle ever turning,
And in the depths of our minds, it's forever burning.

So let us embrace the mystery, the enigma of the
mind,
And explore the depths of psychological time.
For in its winding passages, we may just find,
The essence of our being, beautifully entwined.

Psychological Time -3-

In the realm of psyche, where dreams take flight,
Exists a dimension beyond mere daylight.
Psychological time, a fluid, shifting stream,
Where reality blurs and thoughts gleam.

It's not measured in minutes, nor days gone by,
But in the echoes of laughter and tears that dry.
Each heartbeat a rhythm, each breath a sigh,
As moments dissolve and memories lie.

In the corridors of consciousness, we roam,
Navigating the labyrinth, seeking home.
Past, present, future, intertwined,
In the tapestry of the human mind.

It's the anticipation of what's to come,
The nostalgia of days already spun.
A journey through the psyche's expanse,
Where the clock's ticking holds no stance.

So let us surrender to this timeless space,
Embrace the chaos, let our spirits chase.
For in the depths of psychological time,
We discover the essence of our prime.

Time and Love -1-

In the realm where moments dance,
Time weaves its intricate trance.
A tapestry of fleeting hues,
Love's essence it imbues.

With every tick, a heartbeat's rhyme,
In the grand design of cosmic time.
Moments cherished, moments flown,
In the garden where love is sown.

Through the seasons, love does grow,
In the gentle ebb and flow.
From dawn's first light to twilight's gleam,
Love's tender touch, a timeless dream.

In the hourglass, sands may fall,
Yet love persists, standing tall.
Through the valleys, over peaks,
Love's melody forever speaks.

Time may steal the youthful bloom,
Yet love's radiance fills the room.
In wrinkles etched by years gone by,
Love's flame still dances, reaching high.

For in the symphony of time's embrace,
Love finds its rhythm, its sacred space.
Through fleeting moments, it remains sublime,
The eternal dance of time and love, entwined.

Time and Love -2-

In the silent hush of night's embrace,
Where stars adorn the velvet space,
Time and love, an endless chase,
In the cosmos, they find their place.

In the cradle of the newborn dawn,
Where hopes arise and fears are drawn,
Love's gentle touch, a sacred pawn,
In time's eternal, whispered song.

Through the seasons, hand in hand,
Love's tender bloom, a fertile land.
Time's gentle touch, like shifting sand,
In love's embrace, forever grand.

In the labyrinth of memory's maze,
Where echoes of laughter softly blaze,
Time's gentle hands, in love's embrace,
Each moment cherished, leaving no trace.

In the twilight's shimmering glow,
Where whispers of love softly flow,
Time's embrace, both fast and slow,
In love's eternal, endless show.

For time and love, an endless rhyme,
In the vast expanse of space and time.
Forever bound, in heart and mind,
A timeless dance, forever entwined.

Time and Love -3-

In the tapestry of life, they entwine,
Time and love, a celestial design.
Where each heartbeat counts the chime,
In the grand symphony of love's divine.

Through the fleeting hours, they soar,
Love's tender touch, forevermore.
Time's gentle whisper at love's door,
In every kiss, in every lore.

In the garden where dreams take flight,
Time weaves its threads in the moonlit night.
Love's petals blooming, oh so bright,
In the tender glow of morning light.

Through the storms and gentle breeze,
Time's steady march, love's jubilee.
In every tear, in every pleas,
Love's embrace, an eternal lease.

As seasons pass and ages wane,
Love's flame still burns, a steadfast reign.
Time's gentle touch, a sweet refrain,
In love's eternal, timeless domain.

So let us cherish each fleeting hour,
Embrace the love, feel its power.
For in the dance of time's sweet shower,
Love remains our timeless flower.

Time and Emotions -1-

In the realm where moments blend,
Time dances with emotions penned.
A waltz of joy, a tango of pain,
In the symphony of the heart's domain.

Like sands within an hourglass,
Emotions ebb and emotions pass.
With every tick of the clock's chime,
Feelings swell, then fade in time.

In the dawn's embrace, hope may rise,
As dreams take flight 'neath azure skies.
But dusk descends with whispers old,
And shadows dance where hearts grow cold.

Through laughter's echo and tears' refrain,
Time weaves its tapestry, an intricate chain.
It binds us to the past, guides us through,
A compass for the soul, steadfast and true.

Yet in its ceaseless march, we find,
Moments fleeting, moments kind.
For time, though fleeting, gifts us so,
With memories cherished, love aglow.

So let us savor each fleeting hour,
Embrace the joy, withstand the shower.
For in the dance of time and emotion,
We find the essence of life's devotion.

Time and Emotions -2-

In the realm where time and emotions entwine,
A delicate balance, a rhythm divine.
Each heartbeat a whisper, each sigh a song,
In the symphony of life, where we belong.

Time, the ever-turning wheel,
Guides us through wounds that ache and heal.
Emotions, the colors that paint our days,
In hues of passion, in shades of grace.

In the sunrise's blush, hope takes flight,
As dreams unfurl in the morning light.
But as shadows stretch across the land,
We feel the weight of sorrow's hand.

Through laughter's echo and tears' embrace,
We navigate this ever-changing space.
For time, like a river, flows endlessly on,
While emotions, like waves, rise and are gone.

Yet in this dance, we find our truth,
In moments of joy and moments of ruth.
For time, though fleeting, leaves its mark,
A testament to love, both light and dark.

So let us cherish each passing day,
Embrace the joy, let sorrows sway.
For in the tapestry of time and emotion,
We find the beauty of life's devotion.

Time and Emotions -3-

In the realm where time and feelings meet,
A tapestry woven, both bitter and sweet.
Each passing second, a fleeting grace,
A melody of moments, a dance in space.

Emotions, like stars in the night sky,
Twinkle and shimmer, they soar and they fly.
From the depths of despair to the heights of bliss,
They color our world with their gentle kiss.

Time, the silent witness, steady and sure,
An ever-present companion, forever obscure.
It marches onward, without a pause,
Leaving behind echoes of joy and loss.

In the sunrise's glow, hope finds its voice,
A beacon of light, a reason to rejoice.
But as dusk descends, shadows creep near,
And we confront our doubts, our hopes, our fears.

Through laughter and tears, we journey along,
Captivated by love's enduring song.
For in the embrace of time's endless tide,
We find solace in the moments we abide.

So let us treasure each heartbeat's rhyme,
Embrace the fleeting nature of time.
For in the union of moments and emotion,
We discover life's profound devotion.

Time and Imagination -1-

In the boundless realm where dreams unfurl,
Time dances with the whims of the mind's twirl.
It's there, in the expanse of imagination's flight,
Where moments stretch, and stars ignite.

Time, the silent weaver of destiny's thread,
Entwines with visions in the mind's homestead.
Through the corridors of thought, it wanders free,
Painting tapestries of what could be.

In the labyrinth of memory, it finds its trace,
Etching tales of joy, sorrow, and grace.
With every heartbeat, it whispers its song,
A melody of moments, fleeting and strong.

Imagination, the architect of worlds unseen,
Brings forth realms where time is but a dream.
In the palace of thought, it reigns supreme,
Crafting wonders beyond what eyes can deem.

Together, they dance in an eternal embrace,
Creating galaxies within the mind's space.
For time is but a canvas, imagination its brush,
Painting infinity with every thought's hush.

So let us wander in the realms of our mind,
Where time is boundless and imagination aligned.
In this sanctuary where dreams take flight,
We'll journey beyond the bounds of finite.

Time and Imagination -2-

In the realm where time's river flows,
Imagination's current steadily grows.
It carves through mountains of the mundane,
Creating vistas where dreams reign.

In the hourglass of the mind, sands shift,
As imagination's breeze sets spirits adrift.
Moments stretch, twist, and bend,
In a kaleidoscope where fantasies blend.

Through the corridors of the past, it roams,
Breathing life into forgotten tombs.
Memories blossom, vibrant and bright,
In the garden of the mind's twilight.

Time becomes a canvas, vast and wide,
Where imagination paints its endless tide.
Each stroke a story, each color a hue,
A symphony of creativity, ever anew.

In the tapestry of existence, they intertwine,
As time's steady march meets visions divine.
Together they weave the fabric of fate,
In the grand design where wonders await.

So let us dive into this cosmic sea,
Where time and imagination dance free.
In the boundless expanse of our reverie,
We'll sculpt our destinies, wild and free.

Time and Imagination -3-

In the vast expanse where moments flow,
Imagination's flame begins to glow.
Time, a river, ever winding its way,
While dreams and visions come out to play.

In the depths of night, where stars ignite,
Time pauses, caught in the shimmering light.
Imagination takes flight on wings untamed,
Exploring realms where reality's named.

Through the corridors of history, it roams,
Unearthing tales from forgotten tomes.
With each whisper of wind, each rustle of tree,
Imagination sets the spirit free.

Time becomes a tapestry, woven and spun,
With threads of memories, battles won.
Yet imagination is the artist's hand,
Painting colors across the land.

Together they dance, in a timeless embrace,
Crafting wonders in the endless space.
For where time meets the boundless mind,
There, dear friend, true magic we find.

So let us wander, let us explore,
The realms where imagination soars.
In the endless dance of time and dream,
We'll find eternity in each gleam.

Past, Present, and Future -1-

In the echoes of time, the past does dwell,
A tapestry woven with tales to tell.
Memories linger, both bitter and sweet,
Guiding our steps as we roam and retreat.

Through shadows of yesteryears, we roam,
Tracing the footsteps that led us home.
Lessons learned in the whispers of old,
A treasure trove of stories untold.

Yet the present sings with vibrant hue,
A canvas alive, fresh and anew.
Moments fleeting, like grains of sand,
Slipping through fingers, as we grasp with hand.

Here, in the now, we find our might,
Embracing the day, chasing the light.
For every heartbeat, a rhythm to dance,
In this precious moment, we take our chance.

And what of the future, mysterious and wide?
A horizon of dreams where destinies abide.
Unwritten chapters, awaiting their cue,
A journey ahead, both daunting and true.

With hope as our compass, we chart the unknown,
Carving our path, with courage we've grown.
For time moves relentless, a relentless tide,
But in the dance of existence, we find our stride.

Past, present, and future, intertwined,
A symphony of life, beautifully designed.
Each moment a gift, a chance to renew,
As we journey through time, in all that we do.

Past, Present, and Future -2-

In the whispers of yesterday's song,
Where memories linger, tender and long.
We trace the lines of moments gone by,
In the depths of the past, where shadows lie.

Yet the present beckons with open arms,
A tapestry woven with life's charms.
Each breath a melody, sweet and clear,
In the dance of now, we hold dear.

And what of the future, distant and vast?
A realm of dreams, where hopes are cast.
In the silent embrace of tomorrow's embrace,
We find solace in the promise of grace.

With courage as our compass, we journey on,
Through the trials of time, until dawn.
For in the triad of past, present, and future,
We find the essence of our nature.

So let us cherish each moment we find,
In the tapestry of life, beautifully entwined.
For in the symphony of moments we roam,
We find our purpose, our heart's true home.

Past, Present, and Future -3-

In the vault of memories, the past does sleep,
Where whispers of yesterday softly creep.
Echoes of laughter, tears shed in vain,
In the corridors of time, they remain.

But behold the present, a gift to behold,
With its mysteries unfolding, stories untold.
In the rhythm of now, we find our grace,
Embracing each moment, in its rightful place.

And what of the future, shrouded in mist?
A canvas awaiting the artist's twist.
With dreams as our compass, we set sail,
On the journey ahead, beyond the veil.

In the trinity of past, present, and beyond,
We weave the tapestry of life's sweet song.
Each chapter a melody, woven with care,
As we journey through time, aware.

So let us honor the past, live in the now,
And embrace the future's uncertain vow.
For in this dance of existence, we find,
The beauty of life, in heart and mind.

Mental Time Travel -1-

In the depths of thought, the mind takes flight,
Through corridors of memory, dark or light.
A journey embarked, with no physical trace,
Into realms where time finds its own pace.

Mental time travel, a wondrous art,
Unfolding scenes, stirring the heart.
To days of yore, we softly glide,
Where echoes of laughter and tears reside.

Through misty veils of forgotten years,
We wander, confronting hopes and fears.
Reliving moments, both joyous and sad,
In the theater of the mind, stories clad.

Backward we drift, to childhood's embrace,
Where innocence danced with carefree grace.
Skipping stones on rivers of dreams,
In the meadows of youth, where sunlight gleams.

Forward we leap, to futures unseen,
Where destinies await, in realms serene.
With visions of what may yet unfold,
We navigate the mysteries, bold and untold.

Mental time travel, a timeless quest,
A symphony of memories, ever blessed.
For in the recesses of our mind's domain,
Lies the power to journey, again and again.

Mental Time Travel -2-

In the corridors of thought, I tread,
Where time's illusion softly spreads.
Mental time travel, my vessel unseen,
Guided by whispers of what has been.

Through the mists of forgotten days,
I journey back, in nostalgic gaze.
To childhood haunts, where dreams took flight,
And innocence painted the canvas of night.

In the embrace of moments dear,
I linger, savoring joy sincere.
Laughter echoes in the halls of yore,
As I dance with shadows on memory's shore.

But onward I journey, through the expanse,
Where future's promise begins to dance.
Visions of tomorrows yet to unfold,
In the tapestry of time, stories untold.

With each step forward, I embrace the unknown,
With courage as my companion, I've grown.
For mental time travel, though fleeting and fleet,
Unveils the treasures that make life complete.

So let me wander, through time's gentle sway,
In the realms of memory, night or day.
For in the depths of my mind's endless span,
I find solace and wonder, as a time-traveling man.

Mental Time Travel -3-

In the labyrinth of my mind I roam,
Where time's currents ebb and flow,
A voyager in realms unseen,
Mental time travel, my chosen dream.

I journey back to days of old,
Where memories shimmer, bright and bold.
To childhood's innocence, pure and sweet,
Where laughter echoed with every beat.

Through fields of youth, I softly tread,
Where dreams were spun, and fantasies fed.
In the hush of twilight's gentle glow,
I find solace in the afterglow.

But forward still, my path extends,
To futures waiting around the bends.
In the whispers of what's yet to be,
I find hope's melody calling to me.

Mental time travel, a wondrous flight,
Through the corridors of day and night.
In the vast expanse of my mind's domain,
I find peace and purpose once again.

Time and Eternity -1-

In the realm of fleeting moments, time unfurls,
A tapestry woven with threads that swirl.
Eternity whispers in the cosmic breeze,
A dance between moments, a symphony of ease.

Tick-tock, the clock's rhythmic song,
A journey where seconds and minutes throng.
Yet in the shadows, eternity abides,
A river of moments, where time subsides.

In the hush of twilight, where sunsets gleam,
Eternity's palette paints a timeless dream.
Each fleeting second, a gem in the night,
Yet eternity cradles them, holding them tight.

Through seasons that change, in cycles profound,
Time dances with eternity, a seamless bound.
For in every heartbeat, a universe unfolds,
A story untold, in the tapestry it molds.

A moment's caress, a lingering kiss,
In the arms of eternity, nothing amiss.
Time, a mere chapter in a book so divine,
Eternity's embrace, a love that intertwines.

As stars shimmer above in the vast expanse,
Time's fleeting gaze, eternity's trance.
In the grand cosmic theater, they perform,
A ballet of moments, a symphony warm.

So let us savor each tick, each gentle chime,
Embracing the dance of this cosmic rhyme.
For in the dance of time and eternity,
We find the essence of our mortality.

Time and Eternity -2-

Beneath the moonlit canopy, time takes flight,
A journey through shadows, weaving through night.
Eternity's whispers echo in the starry expanse,
A cosmic dance, where moments enhance.

In the tapestry of dreams, where futures entwine,
Time's fleeting whispers, like a soft, subtle sign.
Eternity, a silent witness to life's fleeting art,
A masterpiece painted on the canvas of the heart.

The sunrise, a promise in the arms of the dawn,
Time's gentle caress, as the day is reborn.
Eternity's gaze in the morning's tender light,
A reminder that moments are woven so tight.

Through the seasons, a symphony unfolds,
Time's orchestra playing, as the story molds.
Eternity cradles the echoes of laughter and tears,
In the mosaic of existence, where love perseveres.

On the river of moments, where memories flow,
Time's current carries us, to places we go.
Eternity, a tranquil sea, where echoes reside,
A sanctuary for moments, in its vast, endless tide.

In the quiet of night, when the stars softly gleam,
Time and eternity meet, in a celestial scheme.
A dance of shadows and light, an endless duet,
A poetic ballet, we'll never forget.

So let us cherish each second, each breath we take,
For time and eternity, a cosmic bond they make.
In the dance of existence, where moments unfold,
A timeless story, in the vast cosmic hold.

Time and Eternity -3-

Beneath the arch of twilight's gentle embrace,
Time pirouettes in a celestial grace.
Eternity's whispers linger in the air,
A tapestry woven with threads so rare.

Moonbeams cascade, a silver serenade,
As time and eternity, in shadows, trade.
Each heartbeat a rhythm in life's grand song,
A journey where moments eternally throng.

In the garden of dawn, where dreams take root,
Time's footsteps echo, a silent pursuit.
Eternity's bloom, in petals unseen,
A sanctuary where past and future convene.

Through the seasons' embrace, a dance unfolds,
Time's story scripted, in sagas untold.
Eternity cradles the echoes of our refrain,
In the vast cosmic canvas, a masterpiece plain.

Sunset's brushstrokes paint the horizon's edge,
Time's fleeting kiss, as the day takes its pledge.
Eternity, a silent witness to the ebb and flow,
A timeless river where memories glow.

Stars, like verses, in the nightly scroll,
Time and eternity, an eternal goal.
In the cosmic ballet of light and shade,
A symphony played, as moments cascade.

So let us cherish the dance of the spheres,
Embracing both laughter and silent tears.
For in the union of time and eternity, We find the
essence of life's sweet serenity.

Time and the Universe -1-

In the tapestry of cosmic rhyme,
Time weaves a tale, sublime.
A dance with stars in the vast expanse,
A celestial waltz, a timeless trance.

Galaxies swirl in a cosmic ballet,
Whispers of stardust in the Milky Way.
Time, the maestro, conducts the show,
A symphony of eons, an endless flow.

From the birth of stars to their fading light,
Time paints the canvas of the cosmic night.
Planets spin in an eternal embrace,
In the cosmic ballet, they find their space.

Time's fingers trace the curves of space,
An artist creating, with gentle grace.
Through nebulae and celestial verse,
Time whispers secrets, in the universe.

Black holes sing a mysterious song,
A melody where time seems to prolong.
In the cosmic clockwork, a celestial rhyme,
Time weaves the fabric of space and time.

Astronomers gaze with curious eyes,
As time unfurls its cosmic ties.
Through wormholes and dimensions unseen,
Time navigates the universe serene.

Eons pass like a fleeting dream,
In the cosmic river, a constant stream.
The universe, a celestial rhyme,
Echoes through the corridors of time.

So, in the grand tapestry of space,
Time leaves its mark, a cosmic trace.
A poem written in the stars above,
A testament to the universe's eternal love.

Time and the Universe -2-

Beneath the canopy of night's embrace,
Where galaxies swirl in celestial grace.
A timeless tale unfolds its verse,
Of cosmic wonders, and the universe.

Through the vastness of space, time weaves,
A narrative of stars that the night retrieves.
In the silence of the cosmic expanse,
The universe unveils its eternal dance.

Nebulas bloom like cosmic flowers,
Painting the void with vibrant powers.
In the cosmic theater, a grand display,
Where comets dance and meteors play.

Time, a silent architect, molds the spheres,
Guiding planets through the cosmic years.
Constellations tell stories untold,
In the night's embrace, their secrets unfold.

Beyond the edge of the known and seen,
A cosmic symphony, serene.
Black holes sing with mysterious might,
Echoing through the fabric of cosmic night.

Across the expanse, where galaxies roam,
Time etches tales in the celestial dome.
A dance of light in the vast unknown,
A universal poem, forever sown.

In the cosmic ballet, where galaxies twirl,
Time, the conductor, orchestrates the swirl.
A poem written in the language of stars,
In the boundless cosmos, where wonders are.

So, gaze into the cosmic sea,
Where time and space dance in unity.
A poem unfolds in the cosmic rhyme,
A timeless ode to the universe's prime.

Time and the Universe -3-

Upon the canvas of the cosmic sky,
A tale of wonder, where galaxies lie.
Time, the artist, with a brush divine,
Paints the universe, a masterpiece so fine.

Stars like diamonds, scattered in the night,
Ignite the darkness with their radiant light.
Planets waltz in a celestial trance,
Caught in the embrace of time's advance.

Nebulas bloom, ethereal and bright,
In the tapestry of space, a breathtaking sight.
Time, the storyteller, whispers in the cosmic breeze,
Chronicles of ages, written in galaxies.

Through the fabric of the cosmic loom,
Threads of destiny, past the edge of doom.
Black holes, like poets, speak in riddles,
Time's secrets hidden in their cosmic middles.

In the dance of quasars and pulsars so grand,
Time weaves a poem across the cosmic strand.
Astronomers, dreamers, gaze with awe,
At the poetry of the universe, without a flaw.

Eons pass, yet the cosmic heart beats,
In the vast expanse, where infinity meets.
Time, the architect of this cosmic rhyme,
Crafts a sonnet written in stardust and time.

So, let us ponder the celestial verse,
As the universe unfolds, a blessing and curse.
In the grandeur of space, where mysteries entwine,
Time and the cosmos, in a dance divine.

Time and the Fourth Dimension -1-

In the tapestry of existence, where moments
intertwine,
Time, the elusive weaver, in the cosmic design.
A dance of seconds, minutes, hours unfurls,
A narrative written in the fabric of the fourth dimension
swirls
.

Tick-tock echoes in the corridors of fate,
As past and future converge at this celestial gate.
A river flowing, ceaseless, in the realm unseen,
The fourth dimension whispers of what might have
been.

Chronicles etched on the pages of tomorrow,
A symphony of possibilities, a harmonic sorrow.
Forward, backward, a journey without end,
In the continuum of time, our stories blend.

Moments like stardust, scattered and divine,
Each heartbeat a rhythm in this cosmic design.
The fourth dimension, a canvas vast and grand,
Paints tales of civilizations rising and sinking in the
sand.

Eternal whispers of moments long past,
The echoes of futures in which we're cast.
A dimension beyond our mortal perception,
Time's enigma, a profound introspection.

Yet, within this continuum, a paradox unfolds,
A dance of cosmic forces, a tale untold.
The past, the present, the future entwine,
In the tapestry of time, where destinies align.

So let us cherish the fleeting, embrace the sublime,
In the ever-changing dance of the fourth dimension's rhyme.
For within each moment, a universe we find,
A timeless tapestry, forever intertwined.

Time and the Fourth Dimension -2-

Beneath the celestial canopy, where stars ignite,
In the embrace of the fourth dimension's gentle light.
A realm where time dances, an ethereal ballet,
Illuminating the cosmos in a shimmering display.

Past, present, future, entwined in a cosmic waltz,
A tapestry woven with constellations, a celestial
pulse.
Time, the unseen sculptor, carving paths unknown,
In the vast expanse where the universe is sown.

Moments, like fleeting comets, streak across the
night,
Leaving trails of memories in their radiant flight.
The fourth dimension, a gateway to the infinite,
A realm where existence and eternity meet.

Ephemeral echoes of laughter, whispers of the
breeze,
In the tapestry of time, where moments find ease.
A journey through the ages, a voyage untold,
As the fourth dimension's secrets gradually unfold.

In the twilight of seconds, where shadows gently cast,
A symphony of time, present and future amalgamate.
Eternal is the heartbeat, resonating in cosmic rhyme,
In the ever-expanding canvas of the fourth
dimension's time.

So gaze upon the heavens, where galaxies convene,
Feel the pulse of existence, the cosmic serenade
serene.
For in the dance of time, a timeless truth we find,
In the embrace of the fourth dimension, our destinies
entwined.

Time and the Fourth Dimension -3-

In the tapestry of the fourth dimension's grace,
Time weaves a story, an eternal embrace.
A river flowing, both swift and slow,
Through the corridors where destinies grow.

Each moment a pearl, strung on the thread,
Of past, present, and what lies ahead.
A cosmic dance in the celestial ballet,
Where dawn and dusk forever sway.

Silent whispers of the moments passed,
A spectrum of memories, holding fast.
In the continuum, where existence unfurls,
Lies the secret of the fourth dimension's pearls.

Threads of fate intertwine, delicate and strong,
As the timeless journey sweeps us along.
Eternity's embrace, a tender kiss,
In the fabric of time, where destinies bliss.

Chasing horizons, reaching for the unknown,
In the vast expanse where dreams are sown.
The fourth dimension, an eternal dance,
A symphony of chance, circumstance.

As stars paint stories on the canvas of night,
In the fourth dimension, everything feels right.
Embraced by time's gentle, cosmic art,
We find solace in the beating of our heart.

So let us cherish each fleeting embrace,
In the tapestry of time, a sacred space.
For in the dance of seconds, we find,
A timeless truth, forever intertwined.

Time and Synchronicity -1-

In the dance of seconds and minutes,
A cosmic waltz, unseen and infinite,
Time weaves a tapestry, vast and sublime,
Where synchronicities gently chime.

Through the corridors of fate they glide,
Moments entwined, in the universe they bide,
Threads of destiny, woven with care,
In the grand design, beyond compare.

Tick-tock whispers of the clock,
A rhythm ancient, a celestial rock,
Synchronicities, whispers of the divine,
In the cosmic ballet, where stars align.

A chance encounter, a twist of fate,
Two souls entangled, their destinies innate,
Time's symphony, a harmonious song,
In the vast expanse, where they belong.

As the sun meets the moon in the twilight sky,
Synchronicities unfold, as the moments fly,
Connected threads, through the tapestry of time,
A dance of purpose, a rhythm sublime.

The flutter of butterfly wings,
A ripple effect, as the melody springs,
Coincidences cascade, like a waterfall's flow,
In the river of time, where stories grow.

Synchronicity, a mystical dance,
Where chance and fate find their romance,
In the silent whispers of the cosmic rhyme,
A serenade of moments, transcending time.

So, in the labyrinth of life, embrace the signs,
Synchronicities, where the universe aligns,
For in the ebb and flow of the temporal sea,
We find the magic of serendipity.

Time and Synchronicity -2-

Beneath the tapestry of midnight skies,
Where constellations tell ancient lies,
Time, a river, winding and free,
Unveils its secrets in synchronicity.

Moonlit whispers on a silent night,
Stars conspiring, weaving light,
Moments entwined in cosmic grace,
A dance of destiny, in every embrace.

Through the corridors of chance they glide,
Synchronicities, the universe's guide,
A delicate ballet of fate and design,
Threads of existence, beautifully entwined.

In the quiet spaces where seconds play,
A serendipitous ballet unfolds its display,
Connections made in the celestial dance,
Threads of time in a cosmic romance.

A chance encounter, a fleeting gaze,
A synchronicity, a mystical maze,
Paths converging, like rivers that meet,
In the cosmic script, where destinies greet.

Clocks ticking in harmonious rhyme,
Echoing through the corridors of time,
Synchronicities, like petals unfurl,
In the grand tapestry, a magical swirl.

Whispers of ages in the rustle of leaves,
In the synchronicities, the heart believes,
Time, a conductor of a celestial song,
Guiding souls where they belong.

So, let the dance of moments play,
In the theatre of time, let hearts sway,
Synchronicities, a celestial art,
A symphony of life, a masterpiece's start.

Time and Synchronicity -3-

Beneath the crescent moon's soft glow,
Where whispers of destiny gently flow,
Synchronicities, a celestial ballet,
In the cosmic script, they find their way.

Time's gentle touch, a brushstroke divine,
Painting stories in the starry design,
A dance of seconds, a waltz unseen,
In the kaleidoscope of moments keen.

Through the meadows of possibility,
Synchronicities bloom in fragility,
Butterfly wings, a ripple effect,
In the tapestry where lives connect.

The hands of fate, in an intricate dance,
Waltzing through the realms of chance,
Threads of existence delicately spun,
In the cosmic loom, where destinies are won.

A chance encounter, a quiver in the air,
Synchronicities, beyond compare,
Whispers of serendipity, echoes in time,
A symphony of cosmic rhyme.

In the mosaic of existence, patterns unfold,
Synchronicities, a story untold,
Time's river, flowing with grace,
Carving paths in the eternal space.

Embrace the moments, the signs, the clues,
In the synchronicities, find the muse,
For in the dance of time and chance,
Life's enchanting, cosmic romance.

Time and Healing -1-

In the tapestry of moments, where shadows
intertwine,
There lies the dance of time, a healer so divine.
A silent symphony, a balm for wounds unseen,
Time, the sculptor of sorrows, where healing is
serene.

With each passing heartbeat, a chapter unfolds,
A tale of resilience, in the story time molds.
In the garden of seconds, where seconds turn to
bloom,
Healing petals unfurl, dispelling the gloom.

The clock's steady heartbeat, a rhythm of grace,
Whispers of solace, as it moves through space.
It weaves through the fractures, knitting wounds with
care,
Time, a gentle surgeon, mending the wear and tear.

Through the corridors of minutes, echoes of the past,
A canvas of memories, where healing is cast.
The scars may linger, like echoes of a chime,
Yet time paints forgiveness, with the brush of time.

As seasons unfold, in the tapestry of years,
Time is a remedy, banishing silent tears.
Patience is the elixir, in the healing rhyme,
A melody of restoration, sung by the hands of time.

In the quietude of hours, where echoes softly fade,
Time whispers courage, lifting burdens laid.
It's a river of solace, flowing ever so wide,
Carving valleys of healing on the soul's tender side.

So, let time be the healer, in its gentle sway,
A salve for wounds, as it takes pain away.
Embrace the ebb and flow, like a comforting rhyme,
For in the arms of time, true healing does chime.

Time and Healing -2-

Beneath the moon's soft glow, where shadows gently play,
A dance with healing whispers, where time finds its way.
In the cosmic ballet, where stars shimmer and align,
There blooms a verse of solace, a healing design.

Through the tapestry of midnight, where dreams take flight,
Time tiptoes gracefully, bringing solace in the night.
Moonbeams caress the wounds, as the night unfolds,
A nocturnal healer, where secrets are told.

In the sanctuary of silence, where healing finds a voice,
Time weaves a lullaby, offering a comforting choice.
A celestial embrace, a balm for the soul's ail,
Night unfolds its healing wings, leaving scars to pale.

As the clock hands trace the constellations above,
Time's gentle touch whispers, a symphony of love.
A celestial orchestra, harmonizing pain,
Guiding wounded hearts through the healing terrain.

In the quiet moments of night's tender grace,
Time is a muse, a guardian of space.
With every breath of darkness, a promise unfurls,
Healing the wounds, mending the fractured pearls.

Under the star-studded canopy, where galaxies entwine,
Time dances with hope, a healer so divine.
In the realm of dreams, where healing is surreal,
Nighttime becomes a sanctuary, where wounded spirits heal.

Time and Healing -3-

Beneath the sun's warm gaze, where daylight softly
gleams,
Time strides in golden hues, stitching fractured
dreams.
In the vast expanse of daytime, where shadows find
reprieve,
Healing rays cascade, offering a chance to believe.

Through meadows bathed in sunlight, where
wildflowers sway,
Time paints a canvas of renewal, a brighter, hopeful
day.
With every sunrise whisper, a melody of grace,
Healing unfolds its wings, embracing each scarred
space.

On the clock's face, the hands move in a steady
rhyme,
A dance of seconds, weaving healing through the
sands of time.
In the cadence of daylight, where moments intertwine,
Time is a gardener, nurturing blooms that once
declined.

With the touch of sunlight, wounds begin to mend,
A gentle restoration, a journey with no end.
In the embrace of daytime, where resilience finds its
tune,
Healing blooms like sunflowers, reaching for the
noon.

The warmth of noonday, a comforting embrace,
Time unfolds its blessings, leaving no trace.
In the rhythm of the afternoon, where healing currents flow,
Daylight becomes a healer, casting shadows low.

As the sun descends, painting skies with amber hues,
Time whispers promises of healing, chasing away the blues.
In the tapestry of twilight, where day bids farewell,
Healing continues its dance, a story only time can tell.

So, beneath the sun's radiant glow, where moments gently peel,
Time unfolds a saga of healing, oh so real.
In the symphony of daytime, where hope and sunlight blend,
Healing is a journey, a timeless friend.

The Arrow of Time -1-

In the tapestry of existence, a thread unwinds,
A cosmic dance, where destiny binds.
Through the vast expanse, where stars align,
Moves the arrow of time, a force divine.

From the birth of galaxies to a silent demise,
The arrow advances, a truth that never lies.
Forward it points, relentless and bold,
Marking the stories that the universe holds.

A quiver of moments, both near and far,
Captured in the flight of a celestial star.
Eternal whispers echo, as ages unfold,
The arrow of time, a tale to be told.

In the river of hours, currents swift,
Time's relentless flow, a powerful drift.
Memories etched on the canvas of space,
The arrow of time, in relentless chase.

A symphony of seconds, ticking in rhyme,
A dance with destiny, an unyielding climb.
Through the tapestry, threads intertwined,
The arrow of time, in every heartbeat, find.

Yet in its passage, a beauty untold,
A kaleidoscope of stories, both young and old.
A reminder that moments, like feathers in flight,
Are carried by the arrow, beyond day and night.

So, let us cherish each beat, each fleeting breath,
For time's arrow moves, an inevitable quest.
In the cosmic ballet, where destinies align,
We are but passengers on the arrow of time.

The Arrow of Time -2-

In the garden of moments, where shadows play,
Dances the arrow, in the light of day.
A journey through realms, both distant and near,
The arrow of time, whispers we hold dear.

Born at the dawn, where dreams take flight,
It marches on, through the day and night.
A compass unseen, guiding the way,
Painting the sky with hues of today.

In the tapestry woven with threads of fate,
The arrow we follow, through love and hate.
A traveler in silence, through cosmic design,
Unraveling mysteries, in the grand design.

From the cradle of dawn to twilight's embrace,
The arrow of time leaves its trace.
Moments cascade like a gentle stream,
A symphony of life, a recurring theme.

Through seasons of joy and the storms we weather,
The arrow marches on, binding all together.
It writes the story of our transient climb,
A poet of moments, an artist of time.

In the dance of existence, where echoes persist,
The arrow of time, an eternal twist.
Let us savor the present, embrace the sublime,
For in every heartbeat, we echo the arrow of time.

The Arrow of Time -3-

Beneath the canopy of the celestial sphere,
Whispers the arrow, a cosmic pioneer.
Through the vast expanse, where galaxies gleam,
Unraveling tales, like a timeless dream.

A silent archer, weaving destiny's thread,
In the theater of existence, where life is spread.
From the cradle of birth to the final rhyme,
The arrow of time, an unfathomable climb.

In the symphony of seconds, a rhythmic refrain,
Each heartbeat echoes, a transient gain.
Footprints on stardust, a celestial rhyme,
Marked by the passage of the arrow through time.

It bends the fabric, with a gentle curve,
A silent witness as destinies swerve.
Through the dance of atoms, in the cosmic mime,
The arrow of time, an ancient paradigm.

Yet, in its journey, a paradox unfurls,
For in its forward march, the past it swirls.
Moments suspended in a celestial chime,
A mosaic of memories, shaped by the arrow's climb.

So, let us honor each breath, each fleeting spark,
For the arrow of time leaves its mark.
In the cosmic ballet, where destinies entwine,
We dance with the arrow, through the grand design.

The Illusion of Time -1-

In the tapestry of moments, woven in rhyme,
Dances the illusion, elusive, sublime.
A fleeting specter, a waltz in the air,
Time, the illusion, whispers with flair.

Tick-tock, a rhythm in the cosmic ballet,
Moments cascading, in twilight's array.
An illusion, a mirage, a shimmering stream,
Time, the enigma, in the moonlight's gleam.

Past and future entwine in a dance,
An ethereal tango, a fleeting chance.
The present, a canvas, painted in hues,
Time's illusion, a muse that confuses.

In the morning's embrace and the evening's glow,
Time wears a mask, an illusion to show.
A magician's trick, a spell to bewitch,
The hands on the clock, a mysterious switch.

A river of memories, flowing with grace,
Time's illusion, a delicate embrace.
Yet, is it a river, or a desert mirage?
A puzzle unsolved, a celestial collage.

The pendulum swings, in a cosmic ballet,
Yet, the illusion persists, it slips away.
Ephemeral moments, like sand in a glass,
Time's illusion, a mystery, alas.

For in the stillness, the silence of chime,
Lies the secret, the essence of time.
An illusion, a concept, a dance so divine,
Yet, in our hearts, its echoes entwine.

The Illusion of Time -2-

Beneath the moon's soft, silver glow,
Where whispers of time in shadows go,
A second's illusion, a heartbeat's rhyme,
In the cosmic theater, the play of time.

Through the corridors of night, it weaves,
A tapestry of dreams, where reality cleaves.
A fleeting waltz, a celestial mime,
In the illusionary grasp of the hands of time.

Yesterday's echoes, a distant song,
In the river of hours, we all belong.
Tomorrow's promise, a future climb,
Yet, today is the gem in time's paradigm.

The clock's hands twirl in a quiet dance,
Moments slipping, a fleeting chance.
Illusion's veil, a temporal prime,
In the grand theater of life's pantomime.

Sunrise whispers stories untold,
As the sunset paints memories bold.
Yet, between the dawn and the vesper chime,
Lies the illusion of time, elusive and sublime.

In the garden of seconds, where seconds bloom,
Time, an illusion, a mystical plume.
A cosmic ballet, a rhythm in rhyme,
An enigma eternal, transcending time.

The Illusion of Time -3-

Beneath the cloak of twilight's glow,
Where the river of time continues to flow,
Illusions dance in shadows sublime,
A symphony composed by the hands of time.

Through the veiled curtain of the night,
Past and future entwined in soft light,
In the theater of dreams, a cosmic mime,
The illusion persists, an endless climb.

Moments like fireflies, fleeting and bright,
In the vast canvas of the starry night,
Each heartbeat a note, a melodious chime,
A sonnet written in the language of time.

The clock's steady heartbeat, a rhythmic sound,
Echoes of yesterday, where memories abound,
Yet, the future's whisper, a mystical rhyme,
A dance with illusions, transcending time.

In the tapestry of dawn, a new day unfurls,
An illusionary dance, a dance of pearls,
Embraced by the sun's warm golden grime,
A canvas painted by the brush of time.

Oh, the illusion, a masterful art,
A kaleidoscope of moments, a beating heart,
In the grand ballroom of life's paradigm,
We dance with shadows, in the illusion of time.

Time and Information -1-

In the realm where time and knowledge entwine,
Lies a dance of wisdom, a cosmic design.
For time, the silent river, ever flows,
While information, the whispering wind, it bestows.

In every tick of the clock's steady hand,
Lies the birth of stories, both vast and grand.
Each second a chapter, each moment a verse,
As time and information intertwine, converse.

From ancient scrolls to digital streams,
Knowledge weaves through the fabric of dreams.
It spans the ages, from past to the now,
A tapestry of truth, upon which we vow.

Time, the custodian, keeps records true,
While information, the guide, unveils the new.
Together they shape our collective tale,
As we navigate life's intricate trail.

In the archive of history, stories reside,
Echoes of wisdom, where truths coincide.
Yet in the ever-expanding universe of the mind,
New vistas of knowledge we continually find.

Time, relentless in its onward flight,
Yet within its grasp, we find insight.
Information, the key to unlock each door,
As we seek to understand, to explore.

So let us honor this dance divine,
Where time and information intertwine.
For in their embrace, we find our way,
Through the maze of existence, day by day.

Time and Information -2-

In the boundless expanse where moments unfurl,
Resides the nexus where time and knowledge twirl.
Each heartbeat, a pulse in the symphony of fate,
As information whispers, weaving the great.

Time, the architect of history's embrace,
Carves pathways through the vastness of space.
Its hands, like rivers, etch tales in the sand,
While information blossoms, a garden unplanned.

From the ancient manuscripts to bytes of code,
A spectrum of wisdom in every abode.
In the depths of libraries, secrets lie concealed,
Awaiting discovery, in truths revealed.

Through the corridors of time, we wander,
Seeking the wisdom that time may squander.
Yet in the labyrinth of data, we find,
A treasure trove of insights, to unwind.

With every tick of the clock, a story unfolds,
As the tapestry of knowledge, it beholds.
Time and information, in an eternal dance,
Guiding humanity with each fleeting glance.

So let us cherish this union sublime,
Where time and information intertwine.
For in their union, we find our way,
Through the realms of uncertainty, night and day.

Time and Information -3-

In the ether of existence, where moments reside,
Time and information serenely abide.
Like celestial dancers in a cosmic ballet,
They weave through the cosmos, night and day.

Time, the silent sentinel, marches on,
While information dances to its own song.
Each passing second a whispering tale,
In the grand tapestry of life, they prevail.

From the dawn of creation to the present hour,
They shape the narrative with unseen power.
In the annals of history, their stories entwine,
Guiding humanity through the sands of time.

In the digital age, information flows,
A torrent of data where knowledge grows.
From pixels to pages, it paints our world,
In bytes and bits, its flag unfurled.

Yet amidst the chaos, a rhythm beats,
In the pulse of time, each heart repeats.
For as the ages ebb and flow,
In the dance of existence, they bestow.

So let us honor this timeless dance,
Where time and information find their trance.
For in their union, we find our way,
Through the mysteries of life, come what may.

Time in Paradise -1-

In paradise, where time's embrace
Unfurls its wings in gentle grace,
The sun, a sovereign in the sky,
Paints golden hues, where dreams can fly.

Eternal moments softly dance,
In nature's arms, a timeless trance.
Where whispers of the wind reveal
The secrets time cannot conceal.

In gardens lush, where flowers bloom,
Time's passage fades in fragrant perfume.
Each petal's fall, a fleeting glance,
Yet in its beauty, time's romance.

The rivers flow with rhythmic ease,
Carving paths through ancient trees,
And birdsong echoes through the air,
A melody beyond compare.

In paradise, where time stands still,
Each heartbeat feels the cosmic thrill.
For here, amidst celestial rhyme,
We're lost in love, beyond all time.

So let us linger, hand in hand,
In this enchanting, timeless land,
Where every moment, pure and true,
Is paradise, forever new.

Time in Paradise -2-

In paradise, where time's a stream,
Reflecting skies in azure gleam,
The sands of hours gently flow,
In whispered tides, both fast and slow.

Beneath the shade of palm trees tall,
Where gentle breezes softly call,
The hours waltz in a languid dance,
In paradise's timeless expanse.

Each sunset paints a masterpiece,
A canvas of celestial peace,
Where hues of pink and gold entwine,
In nature's symphony divine.

In paradise, where dreams take flight,
And stars adorn the velvet night,
The moon, a guardian in the sky,
Watches over with a silent sigh.

Here, moments linger, sweet and dear,
Unfettered by the ticking sphere,
For time is but a passing wave,
In paradise, where souls are brave.

So let us savor every kiss,
In this eternal state of bliss,
For in this haven, love's sublime,
A timeless dance in paradise's rhyme.

Time in Paradise -3-

In paradise, where time's caress
Unfurls the fabric of our bliss,
The sunbeams kiss the earth so tender,
In a realm where moments surrender.

Beneath the arch of heaven's dome,
Where whispers of eternity roam,
The laughter of the gentle breeze
Sings songs of everlasting ease.

In paradise, where dreams take flight,
And worries fade in soft twilight,
The rivers murmur tales untold,
In liquid whispers, pure and bold.

Each flower blooms with vibrant grace,
A testament to timeless space,
And birdsong weaves a melody,
That echoes through eternity.

Here, time is but a fleeting guest,
In paradise's endless quest,
To hold us in its warm embrace,
And bless us with its tender grace.

So let us cherish every hour,
In this enchanted, timeless bower,
For in paradise, love's sweet chime
Echoes through the sands of time.

Time and Space -1-

In the cosmic dance where stars embrace,
Time and space, in their endless chase,
Boundless realms, where galaxies roam,
In the silent expanse, they find their home.

Time, the weaver, of moments past,
A tapestry spun, each memory cast,
A river flowing, ceaselessly on,
Marking the path where existence is drawn.

Space, the canvas, where worlds take flight,
Infinite expanse, where day meets night,
Where planets dance in their cosmic play,
And nebulae shimmer in hues of astral array.

Together they mingle, in eternal embrace,
Time and space, bound by no trace,
For in this grand design, they intertwine,
An endless symphony, in the vast divine.

Time whispers secrets of epochs gone by,
While space stretches wide, to the farthest sky,
In this cosmic ballet, they waltz as one,
Infinite and eternal, until time is done.

So gaze upon the stars, with wonder and grace,
As time and space weave their intricate lace,
For in this grand universe, where all dreams trace,
They dance together, in endless embrace.

Time and Space -2-

In the boundless tapestry of night,
Where stars ignite their radiant light,
Time and space converge, entwine,
In a waltz that transcends the confines.

Across the expanse, where dreams take flight,
Time unfurls its wings in endless flight,
While space expands, a canvas vast,
Where galaxies dance, a cosmic blast.

Each moment a flicker, a fleeting glance,
In the cosmic dance, where all advance,
Eons pass, yet still remain,
In the endless expanse, time's refrain.

Through the corridors of space, we roam,
Exploring realms far from home,
Yet time, a constant, a guiding hand,
Navigating through the infinite land.

In the silence of the void, we find,
The beauty of existence, intertwined,
For time and space, forever entwined,
In the cosmic symphony, of heart and mind.

Time and Space -3-

In the vastness where galaxies roam,
Time and space find their cosmic home.
A dance of ages, silent and sublime,
In the tapestry of space and time.

Time, the river flowing ever fast,
Moments slipping into the past.
Space, the canvas, wide and grand,
Where stars and planets make their stand.

Through the aeons, they intertwine,
In a dance that's both yours and mine.
From the birth of stars to their final breath,
Time and space weave life and death.

In the depths of space, where wonders lie,
And the echoes of the universe sigh,
We glimpse the secrets that they hold,
In the stories that time and space unfold.

So let us ponder, let us embrace,
The mysteries of time and space.
For in their union, we find our place,
In the endless expanse of grace.

Time and Free Will -1-

In the tapestry of time, we weave our fate,
Yet within its threads, free will does abate.
For time, the silent sentinel, marches on,
While we, mere mortals, dance to its song.

Choices flutter like leaves in autumn's breeze,
Each one a ripple in life's endless seas.
But do we truly steer our own course,
Or are we but players in a grander force?

Time's hands tick onward, relentless and true,
As we grapple with decisions old and new.
Do we shape our destiny with every choice,
Or are we bound by time's unyielding voice?

In the expanse of eternity, we stand,
Mere moments slipping through our grasp like sand.
Yet within each fleeting second, there lies,
A spark of freedom, a chance to rise.

For time may dictate the where and when,
But our wills determine how and then.
In the dance of existence, we find our art,
Navigating the labyrinth of heart.

So let us embrace the passage of time,
With courage and conviction, we shall climb.
For though its currents may sway and bend,
In the end, our free will shall transcend.

Time and Free Will -2-

In the boundless realm where time does roam,
Our choices carve a path, a sacred tome.
Free will, a beacon in the cosmic stream,
A flicker of light in the eternal dream.

With each dawn's kiss and each dusk's embrace,
We navigate this maze, this wondrous space.
Time's symphony plays, a melody divine,
Yet in its cadence, our spirits intertwine.

Through the valleys of uncertainty we tread,
With courage as our compass, fears are shed.
For in the tapestry of fate and chance,
We find our strength, our true romance.

Time, the silent witness to our plight,
A canvas for our dreams, both day and night.
But in its vastness, we hold the key,
To shape our destinies, to set us free.

So let us seize each moment, bold and true,
Embrace the power that within us brews.
For in the dance of time, we find our will,
A force that echoes through eternity still.

Time and Free Will -3-

In the realm where time and free will meet,
Our destinies intertwine, a dance so sweet.
For time, the river flowing endlessly,
And free will, the wind that sets us free.

In the tapestry of moments, we are weavers,
Crafting our lives with choices, believers.
Each decision a brushstroke on life's canvas,
Painting our stories with boldness and balance.

Time's gentle whispers guide our way,
As we navigate the currents, night and day.
Yet in the silence, our voices rise,
Defining our paths beneath vast skies.

With every heartbeat, a rhythm anew,
We carve our essence, our dreams pursue.
For in the nexus of time and will,
Lies the power to shape, to fulfill.

So let us embrace this gift we hold,
The power to choose, to be bold.
For in the tapestry of fate, we find,
The beauty of free will, our hearts aligned.

Time and Prophecy -1-

In the realm where moments weave their dance,
And destiny's whispers in each chance,
There dwells the elusive, the grand design,
In the tapestry of time, where prophecies shine.

Time, the silent river flowing,
Carries tales of fate, ever-growing.
In its currents, prophecy is bound,
Echoes of the future, profound.

Through veils of mist and shadows deep,
The seer's gaze, in visions, sweep.
They glimpse the threads of what may be,
In the cosmic tapestry, they see.

From ancient scrolls to whispered lore,
Prophecies speak of what's in store.
A flicker of insight, a glimpse of the divine,
In the labyrinth of time, they intertwine.

Yet, time is a riddle, a paradox untold,
Unfolding mysteries, both young and old.
For even as prophecies are foretold,
Free will's touch can alter the mold.

So we journey on this path unknown,
With seeds of fate within us sown.
In the dance of time, we play our part,
Navigating the labyrinth of heart.

With every step, we shape the course,
Writing our own prophecy, with force.
For in the tapestry of time, we find,
The power to shape what lies behind.

Time, the ever-turning wheel,
Reveals the truth that we must feel.
Prophecy whispers, but it's we who decide,
The story of our journey, far and wide.

Time and Prophecy -2-

In the depths of time's vast expanse,
Lies the mystic realm of prophecy's trance.
Where whispers echo from ages gone by,
And futures unfold beneath the sky.

In the hush of night, when stars align,
Visions dance in the seer's mind.
They see the patterns, the cosmic rhyme,
In the ebb and flow of the eternal chime.

Time, the silent witness to all,
Hears the prophet's whispered call.
Through the corridors of fate, they tread,
Where the past and future are wed.

In ancient tomes and sacred lore,
Prophecies dwell, forevermore.
They speak of kingdoms rise and fall,
Of heroes answering destiny's call.

Yet, in the tapestry of time's design,
Lies the mystery of the human spine.
For though prophecies may guide our way,
It's our choices that shape the day.

With each passing moment, we carve our path,
Facing the future, embracing its wrath.
For in the dance of time, we hold the key,
To unlock the secrets of destiny.

So let us journey with hearts aflame,
Embracing the unknown without shame.
For in the whispers of prophecy's rhyme,
We find the courage to seize our time.

Time and Prophecy -3-

In the whispers of the ancient trees,
And the whispers carried by the breeze,
Lies the tale of time's unfolding grace,
And the shadows of the future's face.

Prophecy, a silent song,
Echoes through the ages long.
It whispers secrets, yet untold,
In the language of the bold.

From the depths of ancient lore,
To the seer's gaze, forevermore,
Threads of destiny intertwine,
In the tapestry of time divine.

Through the veil of mist and dream,
Prophecies dance in moonlight's gleam.
They speak of kingdoms rise and fall,
And of heroes answering the call.

Yet, in the midst of prophecy's sway,
Lies the choice of night or day.
For though the future may be foreseen,
It's our actions that define the scene.

With each moment that we hold,
We shape the story, brave and bold.
For in the dance of time's embrace,
We find the power to leave our trace.

So let us journey, hand in hand,
Through the shifting grains of sand.
For in the whispers of prophecy's rhyme,
We find the courage to embrace our time.

Time and Clocks -1-

In the realm where seconds dance,
And minutes weave their rhythmic trance,
There lies a world of ticking grace,
Where time unfolds in measured space.

A clock, a guardian of the hours,
Its hands, like artists, paint in flowers.
With each tick and tock, a story's told,
Of moments cherished, and dreams untold.

The pendulum swings, a metronome,
A heartbeat echoed in a silent dome.
Time, the maestro of life's grand show,
Directs the symphony as moments grow.

In the morning light or twilight's gleam,
Clocks whisper secrets, a timeless theme.
Their hands, like dancers, gracefully glide,
Through the tapestry where memories reside.

The past, a shadow on the clock's face,
The future, a mystery, a distant chase.
Yet, in this present, where moments unfold,
Time weaves a tapestry of silver and gold.

But do not fear the relentless beat,
For time's embrace is bittersweet.
In every second, a chance to restart,
A canvas painted with the hues of the heart.

So, let the clocks sing their rhythmic song,
As time, the river, rushes along.
In the symphony of seconds, let's play our part,
And savor the dance of the beating heart.

Time and Clocks -2-

Beneath the moon's soft, silver glow,
A tale unfolds, of time's ebb and flow.
In the quiet night, where stars align,
A poem of the cosmos, a celestial design.

Clocks may tick, in the world's steady rhyme,
Yet in the cosmic ballet, a different time.
Galaxies whirl in a celestial trance,
A timeless waltz, where stars advance.

Each moment a twinkle, in the vast expanse,
A dance of stardust, a cosmic dance.
In the night sky's theater, a silent play,
Time weaves constellations in the Milky Way.

The sun and moon, partners in the sky,
Chase each other as the days go by.
A cosmic clock, with hands unseen,
Marks the rhythm where worlds convene.

Celestial bodies in orbits wide,
Tell stories of the universe, far and wide.
Planets pirouette in cosmic delight,
As time dissolves in the soft starlight.

Oh, the cosmic clock, with hands untold,
In the universe's vastness, a story unfolds.
Beyond the ticking of earthly clocks,
Time dances freely in celestial blocks.

So, gaze into the night, with wonder untold,
As the cosmic poem in the heavens is scrolled.
In the timeless tapestry of the cosmic rhyme,
A celestial ballet, where all stars chime.

Time and Clocks -3-

Beneath the boughs of ancient trees,
Where whispers of the wind appease,
A timeless tale unfolds, untold,
In the heart of nature, where stories hold.

The sun, a golden timekeeper's kiss,
Caresses leaves in a soft abyss.
And in the dance of shadows cast,
Time surrenders to the moment's grasp.

Birds, like notes in nature's song,
Chirp and trill the hours along.
Their melodies, a fleeting grace,
Echoes of time in a serene space.

The river, a ribbon of liquid time,
Meanders through hills, a rhythmic rhyme.
Its gentle current, a constant flow,
A liquid clock, where memories grow.

The moon, a nightly timepiece gleams,
Guiding dreams with silvery beams.
Its phases wane and wax, a cosmic rhyme,
A lullaby sung in the language of time.

In meadows where wildflowers bloom,
Time paints petals in nature's room.
Butterflies, with wings so light,
Flutter through time, in fleeting flight.

Nature's clock, in seasons turned,
From spring's embrace to autumn burned.
A cycle ancient, a dance refined,
In the canvas of time, all life entwined.

So, in the heart of the wooded glen,
Listen closely, to time's soft pen.
For nature whispers tales profound,
In every leaf, in every sound.

Time and Digital Watches -1-

In the realm of ticking seconds, where moments intertwine,
A digital dance unfolds, a clock of pixels align.
Time, the maestro, conducts its symphony,
In the digital realm, where watches decree.

Digits illuminate the darkened expanse,
On wrists adorned with a silicon dance.
No ticking hands, no sweeping grace,
Just glowing numbers in a digital embrace.

Blinking colon, a rhythmic beat,
Measuring moments, swift and fleet.
Silent whispers of the digital clock,
In the language of numbers, time does talk.

No gears to turn, no cogs to bind,
Yet time unfurls, a story designed.
Electronic pulses, a heartbeat in code,
In the world of circuits, time is bestowed.

A wrist-bound oracle, a silicon sage,
Counting the seconds on a digital stage.
Precision measured in pixels and light,
In the chronicle of numbers, day turns to night.

Yet amidst the hum of electronic song,
Time persists, steadfast and strong.
In the digital watches, a paradox blooms,
As time marches on in illuminated rooms.

Digits may change, but time remains,
A constant force, no code restrains.
So, in the glow of the digital display,
Moments unfold, swiftly slip away.

In the dance of electrons and numeric lore,
Time and watches entwine, forevermore.
A symphony of pixels, a digital trance,
As time marches forward, in every advance.

Time and Digital Watches -2-

In the kingdom of circuits, where electrons hum,
A digital watch, a keeper of moments to come.
Silent guardian of the temporal stream,
In the digital realm, time takes its dream.

Numbers alight in a rhythmic ballet,
A dance of pixels in the light of day.
No ticking echoes, no mechanical chime,
Yet time unfolds in the digital rhyme.

A wrist adorned with a technological grace,
A glimpse of tomorrow in the present's embrace.
Digits flicker, a cosmic ballet,
As seconds and minutes align in array.

Beneath the glass surface, a world unseen,
Where time is measured in pixels keen.
Binary whispers, zeros and ones,
In the digital watch, the chronicle runs.

A chronometer in a silicon attire,
Guiding us through the electronic mire.
In the language of circuits, a ticking prose,
A digital journey where time ebbs and flows.

Yet, in this dance of bits and bytes,
A reflection of life's fleeting sights.
For time, relentless, marches on,
In the digital watch, an eternal dawn.
In the symphony of code and LED,
A temporal ballet, where moments are wed.
In the heartbeat of pixels, a story told,
Of time unfolding, a tale to behold.

Time and Digital Watches -3-

In the heartbeat of zeros and ones, a digital ballet,
A wrist adorned with a technological display.
In the kingdom of circuits, where time takes flight,
A digital watch, a guardian of the night.

Silent whispers in the binary breeze,
Counting the moments with effortless ease.
No hands to sweep, no gears that grind,
Yet, in the digital dance, time we find.

Pixels shimmer in a rhythmic trance,
A dance of digits, a cosmic advance.
The LED glow, a celestial chart,
Navigating time with a digital heart.

Tick-tock, not in echoes, but in code,
On the wrist, a tale of time is stowed.
Electronic pulses, a symphony of light,
In the digital watch, day turns to night.

Through the circuits and electronic veins,
A temporal journey, where nothing wanes.
In the language of bits, time speaks clear,
A digital oracle, forever near.

Digits change, a kaleidoscope unfold,
In the silicon tale, a story retold.
In the quiet hum of the digital embrace,
Time unveils itself with quiet grace.

So, on the wrist adorned with silicon strands,
A digital poem, where time withstands.
In the quiet glow of the electronic art,
A timeless journey, a beating heart.

Time and Spacetime -1-

In the tapestry of spacetime, a dance unfolds,
A cosmic waltz, where mysteries are told.
Time, the weaver, threads moments with grace,
Entwined with space, in a celestial embrace.

Through the corridors of ages, it strides,
A relentless river where destiny abides.
Eternal echoes of the past resound,
In the vast expanse, where wonders are found.

In the fabric of the cosmos, a story unfolds,
Galaxies spin, as the universe molds.
Planets twirl, in a cosmic ballet,
As time and space unite in a grand display.

Warp and weft of spacetime's quilt,
Infinite realms, where existence is built.
Moments crystallize like stars in the night,
A celestial canvas, painted with light.

Gravity's embrace, a force unseen,
Bends the path where stars convene.
Einstein's whispers, equations profound,
Unravel the mysteries, in spacetime's bound.

Through wormholes and galaxies, a journey untold,
Time's tapestry weaves stories bold.
From the birth of stars to a black hole's song,
In the cosmic ballet, where we all belong.

Yet, in this dance, a truth profound,
Time's elusive nature is rarely found.
A fleeting moment, a cosmic rhyme,
In the tapestry of spacetime.

Time and Spacetime -2-

In the symphony of existence, time plays its tune,
A cosmic melody, from the sun to the moon.
Spacetime's rhythm, an eternal flow,
A cosmic dance where galaxies glow.

Time, the conductor, orchestrates the spheres,
Counting heartbeats in celestial years.
A waltz with gravity, a tango with light,
In the grand ballroom of the cosmic night.

Through wormholes and stardust, we navigate,
A journey through spacetime, our cosmic fate.
Moments are the notes in this cosmic song,
Echoing through the cosmos, where we belong.

Galaxies twirl in a celestial ballet,
Planets pirouette in the Milky Way.
Eons pass like fleeting dreams,
As spacetime weaves its intricate schemes.

Black holes, like poets, scribble in dark ink,
In the vast parchment of the cosmos, they think.
Bending time with a gravitational pen,
Crafting verses that echo, again and again.

Einstein's theories, like verses divine,
Illuminate the secrets of spacetime.
A cosmic poem, where dimensions entwine,
In the cosmic library, where truths align.

In the tapestry of spacetime, we are but a thread,
A fleeting moment, a story unsaid.
Yet, in the grand narrative of the cosmic rhyme,
We dance through the ages, in the embrace of
spacetime.

Time and Spacetime -3-

In the celestial theater, a cosmic play,
Spacetime unfolds in a mesmerizing display.
Time's fingers weave through the cosmic loom,
Creating a tapestry that stretches to the moon.

Through the corridors of eternity, we roam,
Navigating the currents of spacetime's foam.
Each heartbeat resonates with the stars,
In the vast expanse where galaxies are ours.

Warping and wefting, dimensions entwine,
A dance of particles, a cosmic design.
Time, the sculptor, shapes the cosmic clay,
Crafting galaxies in a celestial ballet.

Planets pirouette in the cosmic ballet,
Their orbits traced in the fabric of the day.
Time, the poet, scribes verses in light,
In the timeless script of the cosmic night.

In black holes, secrets are held,
Where spacetime's fabric is tightly swelled.
Gravity bends, distorts the scene,
In the cosmic drama, where worlds convene.

Einstein's legacy, a beacon of insight,
Illuminating the shadows in spacetime's night.
Equations dance with the speed of light,
Unraveling the mysteries, unveiling the might.

In the grand mosaic of the cosmic rhyme,
We are stardust, particles in the sands of time.
Through the vast expanse, our journey unfurls,
In the cosmic ballet of spacetime, we twirls.

Time and Death -1-

In the realm where shadows linger long,
A dance unfolds, a haunting song.
Time, the weaver, threads fate's rhyme,
Entwined with death, a silent chime.

The ticking clock, relentless, cold,
A tale of life in moments told.
Its hands, like specters, grasp and seize,
The fleeting breath, the moments' keys.

In twilight's grasp, the sun does wane,
A metaphor for life's refrain.
Time's gentle whisper, a fleeting breath,
A dance with death, the only death.

Each heartbeat echoes, a fragile beat,
A rhythm played in life's grand feat.
Yet, in the dance, a truth is clear,
Death's not an end, but a frontier.

The seasons change, a ceaseless tide,
As moments bloom and then subside.
With every sunrise, a sunset nears,
As joy and sorrow swap their tears.

In the symphony of life's embrace,
Time and death share a solemn space.
Yet, in the tapestry they weave,
A legacy, eternal, they conceive.

For in the hands of time, we find,
A legacy left, an echo kind.
Though mortal flesh may fade away,
The spirit lingers, a timeless ray.

So, let us savor each fleeting breath,
Embrace the dance, confront the death.
For in the cosmic ballet, we find,
Time and death, in unity, entwined.

Time and Death -2-

Beneath the cloak of midnight's shroud,
Where stars illuminate the cosmic crowd,
There lies a tale of time and breath,
A dance with death, a dance with death.

Through the corridors of fleeting hours,
Echoes the resonance of life's powers.
In every heartbeat, a journey untold,
As time and death their secrets unfold.

Time, the river, ceaselessly flows,
A current that every mortal knows.
Its waves, relentless, sculpt our days,
In a ceaseless chase, a fleeting maze.

Yet, within its grasp, beauty thrives,
In moments shared, where the heart derives
The essence of existence, bittersweet,
A dance with time, a rhythmic feat.

And death, the enigma, the eternal night,
A companion on this cosmic flight.
In its embrace, we find release,
A doorway to a timeless peace.

But fear not the darkness, the unknown,
For seeds of legacy are sown.
In the tapestry of moments spun,
A symphony of life, a setting sun.

With every breath, a defiance to decay,
A celebration of the fleeting day.
In the dance with time, a melody,
A testament to our mortality.

So, let us live with hearts ablaze,
Cherishing each sunlit gaze.
For in the ballet of life's breath,
We find the poetry in time and death.

Time and Death -3-

Beneath the veil of celestial dreams,
Where moonbeams waltz in silver streams,
There lies a tale of time's embrace,
A journey marked by life and grace.

In the tapestry of the cosmic weave,
Threads of moments interlace and cleave.
Time, the sculptor of destiny's clay,
Molding stories in the light of day.

Through the corridors of the ephemeral,
Whispers of mortality, soft and ethereal.
Each heartbeat, a pulsing, rhythmic rhyme,
A dance with time, a fleeting paradigm.

Yet, in the garden where shadows bloom,
Death emerges, a silent, sacred tomb.
A passage to realms unknown, untrod,
A communion with the eternal, with God.

In the grand opera of existence's play,
Characters waltz, both night and day.
Through joy and sorrow, they pirouette,
In a ballet where time and death coquette.

But do not fear the twilight's descent,
For in every end, a new beginning is lent.
A metamorphosis, a cosmic breath,
A seamless union of time and death.

So, let us savor the essence of now,
With gratitude on our hearts, we vow.
In the symphony of life's fleeting breath,
We find the poetry in time and death.

Time and Immortality -1-

In the realm where seconds gently waltz,
And minutes hum a timeless tune,
There lies a dance of fleeting moments,
In the cosmic ballroom, beneath the moon.

Time, the weaver of destiny's thread,
A river flowing, ever forward, never still,
Yet in its ceaseless current, a paradox is bred,
A longing for immortality, an ageless thrill.

Majestic moments, like whispers in the wind,
Painted strokes on the canvas of eternity,
Yet mortals yearn for a pause, a bind,
To defy the clock's relentless authority.

Immortality, a dream that beckons from afar,
A quest for eternal breath, a timeless rhyme,
But time, a master of the celestial spar,
In its embrace, we navigate the paradigm.

Yet, within the echoes of history's rhyme,
In tales of heroes and legends untold,
Lies a glimpse of eternity, frozen in time,
In the hearts of stories, immortality unfolds.

The sun may set, the moon may wane,
Yet echoes of moments linger in the air,
A legacy carved, a celestial refrain,
Immortality found in the stories we share.

So, let us dance within time's fleeting grace,
Cherishing every heartbeat, every chime,
For in the tapestry of moments we embrace,
We discover a semblance of immortality, sublime.

Time and Immortality -2-

Beneath the cloak of night, where stars align,
In the tapestry of time, a poem begins to shine.
Ephemeral whispers of the ancient lore,
A tale of immortality, forevermore.

Through the corridors of ages, shadows play,
Silhouettes of mortals in the sun's array.
Yet in the recesses of a cosmic rhyme,
A yearning for eternal, beyond the bounds of time.

Celestial symphonies serenade the years,
A dance of light, dispelling mortal fears.
The moon, a witness to each fleeting breath,
In its soft glow, the whispers of life and death.

In the garden of eternity, flowers bloom,
Petals of moments, in the vast cosmic room.
Yet mortals crave a timeless embrace,
To transcend the limits, find a sacred space.

Oh, elusive immortality, a poet's dream,
Written in stardust, in the moonbeam.
Yet in the verses of each fleeting song,
A glimpse of forever, where we all belong.

Through the sands of time, we leave our trace,
A legacy woven in the fabric of space.
In the book of existence, each page turned,
The immortality we seek, in lessons learned.

So, let us savor the sweetness of the fleeting,
Embrace the now, without regret or repeating.
For in the dance of seconds, forever lies,
A timeless spirit, within mortal eyes.

Time and Immortality -3-

Beneath the arch of heaven's grand design,
A sonnet whispers in the hands of time.
Through realms of dreams and shadows cast,
A poem of immortality, ever steadfast.

In the embers of twilight, where sunsets bleed,
Eternal echoes in the heart take seed.
A melody sung by the cosmic choir,
A dance of atoms, a celestial fire.

Each heartbeat, a stanza in life's grand verse,
A chance to defy the temporal curse.
Yet, in the vast expanse of the cosmic sea,
Mortality and eternity coalesce, wild and free.

The ancient trees, silent witnesses to years,
Their roots entwined, embracing shared tears.
In the dance of seasons, a timeless rhyme,
Immortality painted in nature's paradigm.

Stars above, like words in the cosmic scroll,
Stories of constellations, each a soul.
A mosaic of moments, an infinite art,
In the gallery of time, where all hearts depart.

Oh, elusive eternity, a fleeting quest,
A yearning encoded in every chest.
Yet in the symphony of life's fleeting chime,
A melody of immortality, echoing through time.

So, let us revel in the transient grace,
Each breath, a stanza, in the grand embrace.
For in the poetry of moments, sublime,
We find the essence of immortality, beyond the sands
of time.

Time and Cause and Effect -1-

In the tapestry of life, where moments weave,
Time dances as the silent master, conceived.
Its gentle hand guides fate's intricate course,
Unfolding destinies with relentless force.

Cause and effect, intertwined in its grasp,
Like threads in a fabric, an eternal clasp.
For every action, a reaction untold,
In the chronicles of time, stories unfold.

From the flutter of a butterfly's wing,
To the tempests of change that seasons bring,
Each choice, each deed, a ripple in the stream,
Echoing through time, in an endless dream.

The past, a shadow that lingers and fades,
Yet its imprint remains in the paths we've made.
The future, a canvas waiting to be drawn,
By the hands of time, from dusk until dawn.

Oh, how we strive to capture its essence,
In moments of joy, or sorrow's presence.
But time, like a river, flows ever on,
A timeless melody, an eternal song.

So let us embrace each fleeting hour,
For time is a gift, a delicate flower.
In the tapestry of life, let us play our part,
Knowing that time binds cause and effect, heart to
heart.

Time and Cause and Effect -2-

In the realm where time's elusive dance unfolds,
Cause and effect, a tale of stories untold.
In the endless expanse where moments collide,
A symphony of life, where destinies reside.

With every tick of the clock, a thread unwinds,
In the fabric of existence, where fate binds.
For every action, a ripple in the stream,
Echoes of choices, in the grand scheme.

From the smallest whisper to the loudest roar,
Each moment's echo resonates evermore.
The past, a canvas painted with hues of yore,
The future, a mystery, an open door.

In the tapestry of time, we find our place,
Navigating through moments with grace.
For time is the sculptor, shaping our story,
Guiding us through life's labyrinth of glory.

So let us cherish each fleeting breath,
Embracing the beauty, in life and death.
For in the intricate web of cause and effect,
Time weaves its magic, with every aspect.

Time and Cause and Effect -3-

In the tapestry of time, where echoes softly ring,
Cause and effect intertwine, in an endless fling.
With every beat of the heart, a story's told,
In the grand design of life, where destinies unfold.

Time, the silent conductor, orchestrates the flow,
Weaving moments together, in a rhythmic show.
For every action, a reaction, a ripple's trace,
In the intricate dance, of time and space.

From the whispers of dawn to the sighs of night,
Each fleeting second, a spark of light.
The past, a ghostly shadow, haunting the mind,
The future, a distant horizon, yet to find.

In the symphony of existence, we play our part,
Navigating through time, with a hopeful heart.
For in the dance of cause and effect, we find,
The essence of life, in every design.

So let us embrace each passing day,
In the tapestry of time, let's find our way.
For time is the canvas, where our stories blend,
A testament to the journey, from beginning to end.

Time and Precognition -1-

In the tapestry of time, we weave our threads,
Moments untold, yet future spreads.
Precognition's whispers softly call,
A dance with fate, a rise, a fall.

Time's river flows, relentless and swift,
Yet glimpses of tomorrow, a mystic rift.
In the depths of dreams, or waking sight,
Visions of what may be take flight.

Whispers from beyond, echoes of tomorrow,
In the silence of the night, or the sun's bright glow.
A premonition's touch, a fleeting spark,
Guiding steps through the dark.

Threads of destiny, intertwined and unseen,
A symphony of moments, where past and future
convene.
Time's tapestry, a masterpiece divine,
Each thread a story, each moment a sign.

Through the labyrinth of time, we tread,
With precognition's gift, ahead.
A glimpse, a hint, of what's to come,
Navigating the maze, until our journey's done.

So heed the whispers, embrace the signs,
For time's mysteries unravel in our minds.
In the dance of fate, with steps sublime,
We journey on, through the sands of time.

Time and Precognition -2-

In the realm where time and fate entwine,
Whispers of the future, a mystical sign.
A glimpse of what's to come, a fleeting glance,
In the cosmic dance, we take our chance.

Through the veils of uncertainty, we peer,
Seeking answers in the haze, crystal clear.
Visions of tomorrow, like stars aglow,
Illuminate the path where we must go.

Precognition's gift, a double-edged sword,
Guiding us forward, yet sometimes ignored.
For with knowledge of what lies ahead,
Comes the weight of destiny, heavy as lead.

But still we journey, with hearts alight,
Embracing the shadows, embracing the light.
For time's river flows, relentless and strong,
And in its currents, we all belong.

So let us cherish each moment we find,
For time is a gift, both gentle and kind.
And though the future remains unknown,
We'll face it together, as one, alone.

Time and Precognition -3-

In the whispers of the wind, a tale is spun,
Of time's relentless march, its race unfun.
Precognition's touch, a fleeting grace,
A glimpse into the future's hazy embrace.

In the depths of silence, visions arise,
A tapestry of fate, before our eyes.
The past, the present, the future entwine,
In a dance eternal, sublime and divine.

Through the corridors of time, we roam,
In search of answers, in search of home.
But time, like a river, flows ever on,
And in its current, we're all but drawn.

With precognition's gift, we glimpse the shore,
Yet destiny's secrets, we still implore.
For in the mystery lies life's sweetest song,
A journey of wonder, enduring and strong.

So let us embrace the unknown ahead,
With courage and faith, our fears shed.
For time and precognition, hand in hand,
Guide us through the shifting sands.

In the symphony of existence, we play our part,
Listening closely to the beat of our heart.
For in the rhythm of life, we find our rhyme,
Bound by time's rhythm, till the end of time.

Years, Months, Weeks, and Days -1-

In the dance of time, a cosmic ballet,
Years unfold, a grand display.
They waltz with grace, a measured trance,
A tapestry woven, a fleeting chance.

Months, the chapters in life's grand book,
Each a story, a fresh outlook.
January's chill, a new beginning,
December's hush, an end, a grinning.

Weeks, the beats in the rhythm of days,
A symphony played in life's endless maze.
Monday's start, a hesitant stride,
Friday's joy, a triumphant tide.

Days, the moments we live and breathe,
A canvas painted, a web we weave.
Sunrise whispers hope, a golden ray,
Sunset sighs, memories at bay.

In the garden of time, where moments bloom,
A kaleidoscope of joy and gloom.
Years, months, weeks, and days entwine,
A journey of moments, a story divine.

Years, Months, Weeks, and Days -2-

Beneath the moon's soft, silver glow,
A tale of time, in verses, I'll bestow.
In the quiet night, where dreams align,
A poem weaves through years that intertwine.

Years, the architects of our life's design,
Crafting stories, memories, and a grand design.
They're the artists painting the sky,
With hues of laughter, tears, and the reasons why.

Months, like chapters in a novel unfold,
Each turning page, a story to be told.
January's frost, a crisp, clean slate,
December's embrace, where memories await.

Weeks, the stanzas in life's rhythmic song,
A melody that carries us along.
Monday's hustle, a humble start,
Sunday's calm, a gentle heart.

Days, the verses written on time's scroll,
In the script of life, they play their role.
Sunrise whispers hope, a brand new page,
Sunset sighs, wisdom of a bygone age.

In the tapestry of moments, woven and spun,
Years, months, weeks, and days are spun.
A symphony of time, an endless rhyme,
A poem of life, for now, and all time.

Years, Months, Weeks, and Days -3-

Beneath the canopy of endless skies,
A poem of moments, where time flies.
In the tapestry of days unfurl,
A lyrical dance of the cosmic swirl.

Years, the architects of destiny's arc,
A journey embarked on life's grand park.
They carve the echoes of laughter and strife,
Etching tales on the canvas of life.

Months, the rhythm in nature's refrain,
A symphony playing through joy and pain.
January's frost, a crisp, cold song,
July's warmth, where memories belong.

Weeks, the heartbeat in life's grand score,
A pulse that resonates forevermore.
Monday's hustle, a spirited start,
Saturday's ease, a tranquil heart.

Days, the verses in time's grand rhyme,
A melody echoing through the sands of time.
Sunrise whispers dreams anew,
Sunset hums lullabies to bid adieu.

In the waltz of moments, where shadows play,
Years, months, weeks, and days in ballet.
A poem of life, an ever-changing theme,
A sonnet written in the moonbeam.

Hours, Minutes, and Seconds -1-

In the tapestry of time, a dance unfolds,
Hours, minutes, seconds, stories untold.
A rhythmic heartbeat, the celestial song,
Measuring moments as they journey along.

The hours, like guardians, stand tall and wise,
Each one a chapter, a pleasant surprise.
From dawn's first light to the twilight's kiss,
They weave a tale of joy and bliss.

Minutes flit by, swift as a fleeting dream,
A cascade of moments in the time stream.
They whisper secrets in hushed tones,
Of love, of laughter, of sighs and moans.

Seconds, the pulse of existence so fine,
Tiny fragments of time, a delicate line.
They flutter like butterflies, swift and bright,
In the grand mosaic of day and night.

Each hour, a canvas for memories to paint,
Moments in time, a never-ending quaint.
Minutes, the threads that weave and connect,
Binding our stories, a tapestry perfect.

Seconds, the heartbeat, the rhythm of life,
In their fleeting dance, we find no strife.
For in the tapestry of time, we're woven,
A symphony of hours, minutes, seconds, unbroken.

Hours, Minutes, and Seconds -2-

Beneath the moon's soft, silvery glow,
The hours unfurl, a quiet, rhythmic show.
Minutes twirl, like stars in cosmic delight,
And seconds flutter, weaving through the night.

In the silence of midnight's embrace,
The hours whisper secrets, a celestial grace.
Minutes, like fireflies, illuminate the dark,
A dance of time, an ethereal spark.

Each hour a vessel, carrying dreams,
Through the cosmic river, where silence teems.
Minutes cascade, like a gentle waterfall,
And seconds, a heartbeat, a universal call.

As morning awakens, painting skies with gold,
The hours unfold stories, both young and old.
Minutes weave patterns, intricate and fine,
In the tapestry of time, a design divine.

Seconds, like dewdrops on petals at dawn,
Reflect the essence of moments withdrawn.
Together they dance, an eternal ballet,
A symphony of time, where moments play.

So, let us savor each tick of the clock,
Embrace the hours, let the moments unlock.
For in the dance of time, where life is spun,
We find beauty in the hours, minutes, seconds, as
one.

Hours, Minutes, and Seconds -3-

Beneath the sun's warm, golden gaze,
Hours unfold in a vibrant haze.
Minutes flutter like petals in the breeze,
And seconds twirl, a dance that appease.

In the tapestry of daylight, stories bloom,
The hours' journey, a sunlit loom.
Minutes, like butterflies, flit and play,
A choreography of time in the light of day.

Each hour a canvas, painted with delight,
A symphony of moments, soft and bright.
Minutes, the threads, connecting the scenes,
In the grand mosaic, where time convenes.

Seconds, the heartbeat, in the warmth of noon,
Marking the cadence of a bright monsoon.
They whisper tales of life's swift flight,
In the sunlight's glow, so pure and bright.

As evening descends with a gentle sigh,
Hours turn to twilight, a lullaby.
Minutes linger, casting shadows on the ground,
A poetic echo, where dreams are found.

Seconds, like stars, begin to gleam,
In the velvet sky, a celestial dream.
The dance of time, an enchanting waltz,
In the symphony of life, where every heartbeat calls.

So, let us cherish the daylight's embrace,
Embrace the hours, let time's rhythm trace.
For in the journey of the sun and its arc,
We find magic in hours, minutes, seconds, embark.

Time and Health -1-

In the tapestry of life, a thread of time,
Unfolding moments, a rhythm, a rhyme.
Health, the precious jewel in this design,
A dance with time, a balance we find.

Tick-tock, the clock whispers its refrain,
Seconds and minutes, a relentless chain.
In the garden of wellness, we sow our seeds,
Nurturing bodies, tending to our needs.

The sunrise paints a canvas anew,
A metaphor for health, a vibrant hue.
Each dawn a promise, a chance to restore,
To cherish the vessel, to cherish it more.

Time, the sculptor, chisels away,
Yet in its passing, let health hold sway.
Not as a burden, but a guiding light,
A beacon through the hours, day and night.

Embrace the journey, let wellness unfold,
A tale of resilience, of stories untold.
For in the mosaic of moments, we see,
Health intertwined with time's decree.

Through seasons of change, let us adapt,
A symphony of well-being, never lapsed.
In the ebb and flow, find strength to cope,
An ode to health, a testament of hope.

So as the hands of time continue to spin,
Let health be the melody that we sing.
In the grand tapestry of life's sweet chime,
May time and health forever intertwine.

Time and Health -2-

Beneath the sky's vast, ever-turning dome,
A tale of time and health, let's compose.
With every heartbeat, a chapter unfolds,
A narrative written in pulses, stories untold.

In the hourglass sands, whispers of age,
A canvas of life, a poetic stage.
Time's fleeting verses, etched on our skin,
Yet within the body, resilience within.

Each breath, a stanza in the poetry of air,
Inhaling strength, exhaling care.
Health, the melody that sustains the song,
A rhythm that echoes, steady and strong.

Through the seasons, as moments elapse,
Time weaves its tapestry, leaving its gaps.
Yet in the wellness, a resilient thread,
A safeguard against what time may embed.

In the dance of days, let joy pirouette,
And sorrow's shadows, let them forget.
For health is the compass that guides our stride,
A beacon of balance, a constant ally.

As the clock ticks on, let mindfulness bloom,
A bouquet of choices to dispel the gloom.
In the garden of well-being, tend and sow,
Seeds of self-care, let them gracefully grow.

So let the poetry of time and health entwine,
A symphony composed in the grand design.
In the journey ahead, with each step we take,
May the verses of wellness our spirits wake.

Time and Health -3-

Beneath the canopy of time's embrace,
A dance with health, a delicate grace.
In the tapestry of moments, we weave,
A sonnet of life, where passions breathe.

Tick-tock echoes through the corridors,
A reminder of moments, of open doors.
Yet in the heartbeat, a rhythm unfolds,
A melody of well-being that time holds.

Through the kaleidoscope of days, we roam,
In the cathedral of health, find a home.
A sanctuary where vitality resides,
A fortress against the changing tides.

Seasons change, and shadows may fall,
Yet resilience rises, standing tall.
In the symphony of life, a harmonious blend,
Time and health, steadfast friends.

As the sun paints the sky in hues so bright,
Let wellness be the canvas of our light.
With mindful steps, through the fleeting years,
Embrace the journey, conquer the fears.

In the alchemy of moments, let us find,
The elixir of health, a treasure kind.
A poem written in the language of care,
In the chronicles of time, a legacy rare.

The End of Time -1-

In the silence of eternity, where stars no longer shine,
Where time's relentless march has ceased, and all
that was, declines,
There lies a realm beyond our grasp, where shadows
softly creep,
And whispers of forgotten dreams in endless slumber
sleep.

No sun to warm the barren earth, no moon to light the
sky,
No seasons to mark passing days, no tears left left to
cry.
The rivers have run dry and still, the mountains turned
to dust,
And all that once held life and light has crumbled into
rust.

The songs of birds have long since ceased, the
oceans turned to glass,
The echoes of forgotten tales now lost to ages past.
No laughter fills the empty air, no footsteps mark the
ground,
For time has come to claim its prize, and all that's left
is found.

Yet in the quiet of the void, where nothing stirs or
breathes,
There lingers still a flicker of the hope that never
leaves.
For even at the end of time, where darkness reigns
supreme,
There lies the seed of something new, a whispered,
distant dream.

Perhaps beyond the final hour, a new beginning waits,
Where time will once again unfold and open up its gates.
So let us face the end of days with courage in our hearts,
And know that even in the dark, the light will never part.

The End of Time -2-

In the twilight of existence, where shadows dance and
fade,
There lies the end of time, where all that was will
cascade.
The stars above grow dim, their light a fading ember,
As the universe exhales its final, solemn surrender.

No more shall the seasons turn, nor birds take flight at
dawn,
For time, the silent sentinel, has finally withdrawn.
The echoes of forgotten tales resound in empty halls,
As the fabric of reality crumbles and falls.

Yet in this cosmic silence, amidst the ebbing tide,
There blooms a quiet beauty, where hope cannot be
denied.
For in the ashes of the old, new seeds begin to grow,
And from the wreckage of the past, new dreams will
surely flow.

So let us embrace the end with hearts both bold and
true,
For though the world may perish, our spirit will renew.
And as the final curtain falls on this grand cosmic
stage,
We'll greet the end of time with hope, and turn to the
next page.

The End of Time -3-

In the final moments, when time begins to fray,
And the universe exhales its very last breath of day,
There's a hush that falls upon the earth, a stillness so
profound,
As if the very soul of existence makes no sound.

Stars flicker and fade into the black expanse of night,
Their distant whispers lost in the eternal flight.
No more the gentle rustle of leaves in the breeze,
Nor the laughter of children, nor the songs of the
seas.

Time itself unravels, a thread upon the loom,
As the cosmos succumbs to its ultimate doom.
Yet in this twilight hour, a glimmer still remains,
A spark of hope that flickers, despite the endless
strains.

For in every ending lies the promise of a new start,
A chance to mend the broken pieces, to heal the
wounded heart.
And though the end of time may seem a fearsome
sight,
It heralds the dawn of eternity, where darkness meets
the light.

So let us face the end with courage and with grace,
Embracing the unknown, in this final cosmic race.
For even as the stars fade and the galaxies decline,
The spirit of existence shall endure, eternal and
divine.

Time and Forecasting the Weather -1-

In the tapestry of moments, woven fine,
Time dances, a rhythm, a cosmic design.
A symphony of seconds, minutes, and more,
Unfolding tales, a boundless explore.

Gaze upon the clock's hands in gentle sway,
As whispers of hours chart the passing day.
A meteorologist of celestial grace,
Forecasting the weather, a time-bound chase.

Clouds, like poets, paint the sky with hue,
In meteoric verses, a story to construe.
Wind, the bard, whispers secrets untold,
In the language of zephyrs, mysteries unfold.

Sunrise and sunset, a celestial ballet,
Time's grand choreography, in night and day.
Yet, in the forecast of moments, we yearn,
To grasp the elusive, to comprehend and discern.

Storms may brew with thunder's roar,
As time weaves tales, ancient and folklore.
Raindrops cascade, a rhythmic refrain,
Time's symphony echoing, a celestial gain.

A dance with the seasons, a meteoric waltz,
In the dance of time, every heartbeat exalts.
For in the forecast of life, we find,
A kaleidoscope of moments, intertwined.

So, read the skies with a hopeful gaze,
Forecast the weather in life's endless maze.
For time, like weather, is ever changing,
Yet within its dance, there's beauty engaging.

Time and Forecasting the Weather -2-

Beneath the canopy of celestial art,
Time unfurls, a masterpiece from the heart.
In the alchemy of moments, a poet's grace,
A sonnet written in the cosmic space.

Foretelling tales in the wind's soft sigh,
Forecasting dreams that drift and fly.
Clouds of doubt may shroud the way,
Yet sunbeams pierce, in the light of day.

The weathered hands of time, they spin,
A dance eternal, where beginnings begin.
Through seasons of joy and storms that pass,
Each fleeting moment, a looking glass.

A meteorologist of life, we become,
Predicting tides, beneath the moon and sun.
In the dance of fate, we seek to find,
The patterns etched by hands, unkind.

Yet storms bring growth, and rain, rebirth,
As time orchestrates its cosmic mirth.
Embrace the forecast, both clear and gray,
In every forecast, a chance to sway.

Time, the weaver, of stories untold,
In its tapestry, both young and old.
Tomorrow's whispers, in today's breeze,
Forecasting the future, with subtle ease.

So, let us be the poets of our fate,
Chasing the horizon, before it's too late.
In the dance of time, as moments sever,
We forecast a future, bound forever.

Time and Forecasting the Weather -3-

Beneath the canvas of the endless sky,
Time unfolds, a script we can't deny.
In the alchemy of hours, a tale to tell,
A forecast written, where destinies swell.

The sun, a painter with hues aglow,
Brushing dawn's canvas, a daily show.
Clouds, like poets, weave stories untold,
In the vast tapestry where dreams unfold.

Winds whisper secrets in a cryptic code,
Forecasting whispers on the life's road.
Thunderous echoes, a storm's refrain,
Yet after rain, the earth does regain.

In the dance of seasons, a ballet divine,
Nature's rhythm, a cosmic design.
The meteorologist of time deciphers,
The cryptic verses, the cosmic ciphers.

Moments fleeting, like butterflies,
Yet in their flutter, love never dies.
Forecasting heartbeats, a pulse's rhyme,
In the grand theater of the endless time.

Embrace the warmth of the sunlit ray,
Weather the storms, come what may.
For time, the mystic, with its rhythmic beat,
Guides our steps on destiny's street.

So, in the forecast of life, let's find,
The beauty etched in every kind.
A poem of time, a celestial song,
Where moments dance, and dreams belong.

Time and Youth -1-

In the tapestry of moments, woven with care,
Time dances gracefully, a fleeting affair.
Youth, a melody in the symphony of age,
A chapter written on life's vibrant page.

The clock's gentle whispers, a constant hum,
Echoes of yesterday, where youth did drum.
A cascade of seconds, like grains of sand,
Slipping through fingers, an ephemeral band.

Oh, fleeting youth, like a rose in bloom,
With dreams in your heart, dispelling gloom.
The sunlit days, the moonlit nights,
Chasing after stars, reaching dizzying heights.

In the canvas of dawn, where the sun does rise,
Youth unfurls its wings, a butterfly in disguise.
Laughter like music, echoes in the air,
A tapestry of moments, woven with flair.

But time, relentless, as rivers do flow,
A current that carries, an inevitable tow.
Yet, in the dance with age, a beauty found,
Wisdom emerging, like leaves on the ground.

For every wrinkle, a story to tell,
In the depths of experience, where shadows swell.
Youth may fade like a sunset's glow,
But in the heart's archives, its echoes grow.

So cherish the present, embrace the now,
Let laughter and joy be your eternal vow.
For time may age the body, but the spirit's truth,
Is forever entwined with the essence of youth.

Time and Youth -2-

Beneath the canopy of the cosmic sea,
Time weaves tales of youth, a melody.
In the tapestry of days, where moments twine,
A symphony of dreams, a dance divine.

The morning sun, a golden kiss,
Awakens youth in nature's bliss.
Each dew-kissed petal, a whispering truth,
A testament to the eternal dance of youth.

Through meadows green and skies so blue,
Footsteps echo, dreams anew.
The hands of time, a gentle stream,
Yet youth persists in the heart's gleam.

In the laughter of children, carefree and wild,
In the dance of the wind, a playful child.
Oh, youth, the painter of the canvas of now,
Brushstrokes of joy, on life's vibrant brow.

Chasing butterflies in fields of delight,
As the day unfolds, a treasure trove in sight.
The sunset hues, a palette so bright,
Reflecting the magic of youth's endless light.

In the moonlit serenade, a timeless tune,
Youth dances beneath the silvered moon.
Stars whisper secrets, the universe imparts,
A symphony of ages, intertwining hearts.

Through the ebb and flow of life's grand rhyme,
Youth persists, an everlasting paradigm.
For in the rhythm of time's ceaseless song,
The spirit of youth forever belongs.

Time and Youth -3-

In the garden of time, where memories bloom,
Youth pirouettes, dispelling all gloom.
A carousel of laughter, a carnival of dreams,
In the tapestry of life, where joy redeems.

Each heartbeat echoes a tale untold,
Of adventures in youth, both fearless and bold.
Sun-kissed moments, like petals unfold,
In the meadows of time, where stories are scrolled.

With each sunrise, a promise reborn,
Youth's symphony plays from dusk till morn.
Whispers of wonder in the zephyr's embrace,
A dance with time, an eternal chase.

Oh, to capture the essence of youth,
In the verses of time, where honesty soothes.
A fountain of dreams, an eternal spring,
Where hope takes flight on gossamer wing.

Through the labyrinth of days and years,
Youth persists, conquering all fears.
A treasure trove of moments, sparkling and bright,
In the realm of time, a beacon of light.

For in the heart's chamber, where memories reside,
Youth's flame burns, a steady guide.
Through the kaleidoscope of time's embrace,
The spirit of youth leaves an indelible trace.

Time and Old Age -1-

In the tapestry of time, a tale unfolds,
A journey through years, as life beholds.
Old age, a chapter in the book of fate,
Where echoes of youth slowly dissipate.

Time's relentless march, a steady stream,
Leaves wrinkles on faces, like a silent dream.
Each line etched with stories, wisdom untold,
In the quiet corridors of memories, they hold.

Once vibrant and spry, like the morning dew,
Now weathered and worn, yet resiliently true.
The hands that once held dreams so tight,
Now cradle the echoes of a fading light.

Seasons change, as does the hour,
Yet old age bears a unique power.
A reservoir of moments, a treasury of years,
A testament to laughter, to joy, to tears.

The clock ticks on, an unwavering chime,
Marking the passing of this borrowed time.
In the twilight of life, reflections grow,
A mosaic of experiences, a bittersweet glow.

Yet, amidst the shadows that time may cast,
Old age carries a beauty that will forever last.
A tapestry woven with threads so fine,
A masterpiece crafted by the hands of time.

So, let us honor the elders, the wise and sage,
As they dance with time on this final stage.
For in their stories, in their weathered gaze,
We find the essence of life's eternal maze.

Time and Old Age -2-

Beneath the cloak of time, the years unfold,
A symphony of memories, both silver and gold.
Old age, a canvas painted with grace,
Each wrinkle a line, a life to trace.

The hands that once held dreams so tight,
Now weave through shadows in the fading light.
In the amber glow of the setting sun,
A lifetime's journey, a tale well-spun.

Time, the sculptor of this aging frame,
Leaves imprints of stories, each with a name.
A face adorned with the marks of laughter,
A testament to the years lived after.

The steps may slow, the pace may wane,
Yet, in the heart, a fire does remain.
Wisdom like a lantern, glowing bright,
Guiding through the quiet of the night.

Through the corridors of memory, they roam,
In the sanctuary of years, they find a home.
A tapestry woven with threads of yore,
Whispers of a lifetime, forevermore.

In the embrace of twilight, a quiet grace,
Old age reveals its tender face.
For as the sun sets, and shadows grow long,
It's in the echoes of the past that we find our song.

Time and Old Age -3-

In the garden of time, where moments bloom,
Old age arrives, casting shadows on the room.
A tapestry woven with threads of grace,
A portrait painted in the lines on the face.

The hands, once steady, now tell tales,
Of struggles faced and distant sails.
In the quiet hum of the evening's hush,
Echoes of a lifetime, a bittersweet rush.

Gentle whispers of laughter, like a soft breeze,
Through the branches of a weathered tree, appease.
Fading footsteps mark the well-traveled road,
In the anthology of life, each chapter's told.

Eyes that have witnessed the dance of years,
Reflect the joys, the sorrows, the silent tears.
Yet, in the quietude of the waning light,
There's a resilience, a shimmer, burning bright.

Old age, a lantern in the gathering dusk,
Illuminating memories, a mosaic of musk.
The symphony of a life, played on heartstrings,
A melody that through time forever sings.

So, let us honor the elders, weathered and wise,
For within their gaze, a profound sunrise.
In the twilight of existence, they find repose,
A testament to how each life gracefully flows.

Time and the Elixir of Life -1-

In the tapestry of time, a dance unfolds,
A fleeting waltz, stories yet untold.
Moments woven, a delicate thread,
The elixir of life, where dreams are bred.

Tick-tock whispers the ancient clock,
Through the corridors, time does walk.
A symphony of seconds, a rhythmic rhyme,
In its arms, we sip the sweetest prime.

The elixir of life, a potion rare,
Held within moments, beyond compare.
A sip of sunrise, a taste of twilight,
In every heartbeat, in every starlight.

The past, a canvas painted in hues,
A gallery of memories, where time strews.
The future, a mystery veiled in mist,
Yet present, the elixir we can't resist.

Chasing seconds, like butterflies in flight,
Through the day's canvas, into the night.
Eternal quest for the essence divine,
The elixir of life, in every design.

Oh, the elixir, ageless and pure,
In the laughter of children, in love's allure.
It whispers softly in the winds that blow,
A timeless potion, a constant flow.

But time, a river, relentless it streams,
Carrying hopes, vanishing dreams.
Yet, in its current, a chance to be,
One with the elixir, wild and free.

So, dance in the garden of moments untold,
Cherish the elixir, let it enfold.
For in the tapestry of time, we find,
The elixir of life, forever entwined.

Time and the Elixir of Life -2-

Beneath the cloak of night, where shadows play,
A tale of time unfolds, in the cosmic ballet.
Stars shimmer, witness to life's grand mime,
As we seek the elusive elixir, a dance through time.

In the realm of dreams, where wishes soar,
We glimpse the elixir, on the distant shore.
Whispers of ages echo in the cosmic rhyme,
A celestial rhythm, a dance through time.

Through the corridors of yesterday, echoes linger,
Each step a note, every heartbeat a singer.
In the book of moments, a narrative sublime,
We sip the elixir, a dance through time.

The past, a lantern casting shadows long,
Yet in its glow, we find where we belong.
Lessons etched like verses in a poetic chime,
A ballad of wisdom, a dance through time.

Tomorrow's canvas, blank and undefined,
A palette waiting for colors to be entwined.
In the brushstrokes of fate, a pantomime,
Painting the elixir, a dance through time.

Moments crystallize, like dew on dawn's embrace,
Each one a jewel, a memory to trace.
In the mosaic of existence, a paradigm,
We drink the elixir, a dance through time.

Oh, the elixir, a potion of grace,
In the laughter of now, in love's embrace.
Through the tapestry of existence, we climb,
Guided by the elixir, a dance through time.

So let us savor this cosmic ballet,
In the symphony of moments, find our way.
Eternal voyage, a rhythm so sublime,
In the dance of existence, through the elixir of time.

Time and the Elixir of Life -3-

Beneath the moon's soft glow, a serenade,
A poem of existence, in twilight's cascade.
Through the veil of night, where stars align,
A poetic dance, the elixir of life does entwine.

In the quiet whispers of a midnight breeze,
Echoes the symphony of time with ease.
A celestial ballet, a cosmic rhyme,
Unfolding mysteries in the elixir of time.

Moonbeams weave tales, silver and bright,
Casting shadows that dance in the night.
A celestial waltz, a rhythm divine,
In the heart's chamber, the elixir does shine.

Each heartbeat echoes in the cosmic song,
A melody where life and time belong.
In the ink of night, where dreams mime,
We're dancers in the elixir, a dance through time.

Tomorrow's horizon, a canvas yet untouched,
With hues of hope, dreams deeply clutched.
In the tapestry of fate, a design,
We seek the elixir, a dance through time.

Embraced by moments, both sweet and sorrowed,
We find solace in today, our spirits borrowed.
A fleeting journey, a paradigm,
Drinking the elixir, a dance through time.

So, let us twirl in the moonlit glow,
Cherish the moments as they ebb and flow.
In life's grand ballroom, with steps so prime,
We dance in the elixir, a dance through time.

The Flow of Time -1-

In the river of existence, where moments gently
stream,
A timeless dance of moments, in the flow of time, we
dream.
From the dawn's first blush to the evening's serene
chime,
Life unfolds its tapestry in the ever-rolling rhyme.

A river of seconds, a cascade of years,
Each fleeting moment, shedding joy and tears.
The past, a distant echo, a whisper in the breeze,
As the present moment unfolds, with graceful ease.

In the garden of memories, flowers bloom and fade,
Petals of yesterday in the river cascade.
The future, a misty horizon, yet to be unveiled,
A canvas of dreams, where hopes are gently nailed.

The clock's relentless ticking, a heartbeat of the earth,
A rhythmic pulse that marks each precious birth.
As seasons change and shadows climb,
We sail along the river, in the vessel of time.

Eternal in its essence, yet ever on the move,
Time weaves its story, a tapestry of love.
Moments intertwined, like a celestial rhyme,
In the timeless river, we journey through time.

Cherish each ripple, each current, each tide,
For in the river of time, our destinies reside.
Embrace the fleeting seconds, hold them like gold,
For in the flow of time, life's stories are told.

The Flow of Time -2-

Beneath the moon's soft glow, the night unfurls,
A cosmic ballet, where time twirls.
Stars adorn the velvety tapestry above,
Whispering tales of the universe, stories of love.

In the silent hours, when shadows dance,
Time takes on a mystical, ethereal trance.
The clock's hands move in a moonlit rhyme,
As dreams unfold in the corridors of time.

Midnight, a portal to the realm unseen,
Where fantasies bloom and realities glean.
A celestial waltz, in the cosmic ballet,
Where wishes are woven, as stardust at play.

The owl's hoot, a nocturnal song,
As the river of time continues to throng.
Echoes of yesterday, like ripples in a pond,
Merge with the present, in the night beyond.

The pendulum swings, a metronome of fate,
Yet, in the darkness, we navigate.
Through the veiled hours, where seconds chime,
We find our way in the labyrinth of time.

Morning's first light, a herald reborn,
Breaking the silence, a brand-new morn.
Yet, the echoes linger, in the dawn's soft hue,
As the journey of time unfolds anew.

So, dance in the moonlight, embrace the night,
In the symphony of time, find your light.
For in the cosmic dance, where stars align,
We're but travelers, in the grand design.

The Flow of Time -3-

Beneath the boughs of ancient trees, where whispers weave,
A symphony of nature, where time does cleave.
Leaves rustle softly in the breeze's embrace,
A dance of moments, a tranquil space.

The sun, a painter, strokes the sky with hues,
A canvas of dawn, where morning renews.
Mountains stand as sentinels, timeless and tall,
Witnessing the cascade, the seasons' gentle fall.

Rivers meander through valleys wide,
Carving stories in the earth's silent guide.
In the heart of the forest, where time is unfurled,
A sanctuary of echoes, a shelter for the world.

The meadows bloom with flowers bright,
Petals of joy catching the sun's warm light.
A melody of birdsong, a timeless rhyme,
In nature's embrace, we transcend time.

Clouds drift lazily, a celestial ballet,
Painting stories on the canvas of the day.
The moon, a guardian in the velvet night,
Guides us through darkness with gentle light.

In the tapestry of nature, woven with care,
Time is a river, flowing everywhere.
A continuum of moments, a harmonious chime,
In the embrace of Earth, we find the sublime.

So, let us wander, beneath the sky's dome,
In nature's cathedral, we find our home.
For in the quiet whispers of wind and pine,
We touch the eternal, in the flow of time.

Time and Destiny -1-

In the tapestry of fate, where moments weave,
Time dances, a cosmic rhythm to perceive.
A river flowing, relentless and free,
Carving destiny, a tale for you and me.

Through the ticking of clocks, in silent grace,
Destiny unfolds, a delicate embrace.
Threads of time entwine, a delicate ballet,
Weaving dreams, in the night and day.

From the first breath to the final sigh,
Destiny whispers, reaching for the sky.
A dance with time, a waltz so divine,
Guiding our steps, along the grand design.

The past, a canvas painted with yesteryears,
The present, a gift, easing both hopes and fears.
Tomorrow's secrets held in time's embrace,
Destiny's hand guiding with gentle grace.

Moments like stardust, shimmer and gleam,
In the vast cosmos, where dreams redeem.
Time's tapestry, a masterpiece untold,
Destiny's script in letters of gold.

Chasing the sunrise, and the setting sun,
In the tapestry of time, our stories are spun.
A journey intertwined, a destiny we chase,
Guided by time, in its infinite grace.

Yet, within this dance, a choice to be,
An architect of fate, shaping destiny.
For time and destiny, a partnership grand,
In the palm of our hands, like grains of sand.

So, let us savor each moment's kiss,
As time and destiny merge in bliss.
For in the symphony of life's grand rhyme,
We find our purpose, transcending time.

Time and Destiny -2-

Beneath the canopy of the celestial dome,
Where stars converse and galaxies roam.
A tale unfolds, woven in destiny's rhyme,
A cosmic ballet, a dance through time.

Through the eons, where seconds unfold,
A story written in stardust, ancient and bold.
Time, the weaver, with threads unseen,
Destiny's choreography, a celestial sheen.

In the realm of dawn and twilight's glow,
Destiny's whispers, soft and slow.
A journey scripted on the parchment of the sky,
Time's silent witness, as moments fly.

A dance of shadows, in the moon's soft glow,
Destiny's rhythm, a mystical flow.
The past, a constellation of memories bright,
Time's canvas painted in the softest light.

On the wings of hours, destiny takes flight,
A comet's trail, burning through the night.
Through valleys of joy and mountains of sorrow,
Time's echo lingers, a promise for tomorrow.

In the tapestry of existence, threads entwine,
Destiny's design, a cosmic design.
Embraced by the stars, kissed by the moon,
Time's eternal heartbeat, a timeless tune.

So, as the sun sets and the stars align,
In the symphony of life, let our spirits shine.
For in the dance of time and destiny's grace,
We find our place, a celestial embrace.

Time and Destiny -3-

In the hush of twilight, where shadows play,
Time and destiny waltz in the fading day.
A symphony of moments, a celestial rhyme,
In the dance of existence, a rhythm divine.

Through the corridors of fate, we navigate,
On the wings of hours, we contemplate.
Destiny's tapestry, a canvas unfurled,
Time's embrace, a journey through the world.

Moments flutter like butterflies in the breeze,
Destiny's whispers through rustling leaves.
A chapter written in the book of hours,
As time weaves tales from fragrant flowers.

Sunrise paints the sky in hues so bold,
Destiny's secrets in each story told.
In the hands of time, the future's mold,
A destiny awaiting, yet to be unfold.

Stars above, like beacons in the night,
Guide our steps through the silent plight.
Destiny's constellations, a map so clear,
In the vast expanse, we conquer fear.

Time's river flows, a relentless stream,
Carrying hopes and dreams, a boundless theme.
Destiny's compass, pointing the way,
Through the cycles of night and day.

So, let us dance in the cosmic embrace,
Time and destiny, an eternal chase.
In the tapestry of life, woven and spun,
A poem written, a journey begun.

Time and Creation -1-

In the tapestry of existence, a thread unfolds,
Time's gentle fingers weave stories untold.
Creation, a dance in the cosmic expanse,
A symphony of moments, a fleeting chance.

The clock ticks, a rhythmic heartbeat,
Echoes of eternity, where destinies meet.
In the tapestry of time, a canvas so vast,
Creation's whisper, a spell it cast.

From the womb of silence, galaxies birthed,
A cosmic dance, where stardust swirled.
Planets pirouette in celestial delight,
Creation unfolds, a breathtaking sight.

Through the corridors of ages, a river flows,
Time's current carries the seeds it sows.
A painter's palette, colors unfurl,
Creation's canvas, a majestic swirl.

In the quiet of dawn, a sunrise begins,
A masterpiece painted with hues that win.
Mountains rise, oceans embrace,
Creation's rhythm, an eternal grace.

From the first breath to the final sigh,
Time's story echoes in the vast sky.
Creation's tale, a narrative divine,
A journey through epochs, an intricate design.

Yet, in the dance of seconds, moments fleeting,
Time's melody, an eternal greeting.
Creation whispers in the wind's soft kiss,
A timeless dance, an everlasting bliss.

Time and Creation -2-

Beneath the cloak of midnight's embrace,
Where stars ignite and dreams take place,
Time weaves a tale, a cosmic rhyme,
A symphony of creation in the vast chime.

In the womb of silence, a spark unfolds,
A genesis story, as the universe molds.
From whispers of atoms to galaxies afar,
Time dances, a celestial avatar.

Through the eons, a cosmic ballet,
Creation pirouettes in the Milky Way.
Planets waltz in orbits, a cosmic trance,
Time's heartbeat in the celestial expanse.

In the realm of dawn, where day is born,
Creation stretches, a canvas adorned.
Sunrise paints the skies with hues so bright,
A palette of wonder, morning's first light.

Mountains rise, their peaks touch the sky,
Time carves valleys as the rivers sigh.
Creation's fingerprint on every land,
A masterpiece crafted by Time's own hand.

Through the cycles, seasons ebb and flow,
Creation's tapestry continues to grow.
From bud to bloom, life's endless song,
Time, the conductor, where moments belong.

In the quiet hush of a moonlit night,
Creation whispers, a soft delight.
Stars shimmer in a cosmic ballet,
Time's cadence, guiding each astral play.

From the cradle of birth to the silence of sleep,
Time is the river, flowing deep.
Creation's story, a lyrical rhyme,
In the boundless embrace of the infinite time.

Time and Creation -3-

Beneath the cloak of twilight's glow,
Where shadows dance, and whispers grow,
Time unfurls its wings, a silent flight,
In the canvas of creation, bathed in soft moonlight.

A symphony of moments, each a fleeting note,
In the cosmic sonata, where galaxies float.
Creation, a poet, weaving verses in the night,
As constellations twinkle, in celestial light.

In the garden of dreams, where thoughts take root,
Time tends to seeds, bearing stories to fruit.
Petals of potential bloom with grace,
Creation's garden, a sacred space.

Through the corridors of yesterday and tomorrow,
Time's river flows, a perpetual sorrow.
Creation's echo, a melody in the breeze,
Leaves rustle, revealing life's mysteries.

Mountains stand as ancient witnesses,
Silent sentinels to time's caresses.
Creation sculpted in the rugged stone,
A testament to moments, engraved and honed.

The dance of atoms, a cosmic ballet,
In the theater of existence, night and day.
Time orchestrates, a conductor unseen,
Creation's anthem, in the celestial scene.

From the dawn's first blush to the dusk's embrace,
Creation unfolds, an eternal grace.
In the tapestry of time, every thread weaves,
A poem of life, in the heart that believes.

So, in this cosmic dance, where moments entwine,
Let us savor the verses, the rhythm divine.
For in the poetry of time, we find our part,
A symphony of creation, a work of art.

Time and Evolution -1-

In the dance of ages, time unfolds,
A tapestry of stories, untold.
From the dawn of existence, a cosmic spark,
Evolution's journey, leaving its mark.

Through eons vast, a relentless stream,
Time weaves a tale, like a vivid dream.
From primordial seas to towering trees,
Life evolves with gentle ease.

In the ancient embrace of Earth's domain,
Time whispers secrets, a silent refrain.
Microscopic wonders to giants in flight,
Evolution paints the canvas of the night.

From finned creatures to creatures with wings,
Time orchestrates the symphony it brings.
Adaptation's dance, survival's song,
In the melody of ages, we all belong.

Through epochs and eras, a constant flow,
Time molds the future, let it be known.
Creatures arise and others depart,
A timeless rhythm, a beating heart.

Humanity's chapter, a recent page,
In the grand book of time, a fleeting stage.
We stand on the shoulders of ancient kin,
Witnessing the tale as it begins.

Through the cycles of seasons and celestial sway,
Time is the sculptor, shaping the clay.
In the cosmic dance, a timeless art,
Evolution and time, never apart.

As the clock ticks on, a relentless chime,
A dance of seconds, a fleeting rhyme.
Embrace the journey, let your spirit revolve,
For in the hands of time, we all evolve.

Time and Evolution -2-

Beneath the canopy of endless night,
Time weaves a tapestry, pure and bright.
From stardust born, a cosmic serenade,
Evolution's dance, a grand charade.

Through epochs vast, the world transforms,
A symphony of life in varied forms.
From feathered skies to depths below,
Time's cadence, an eternal flow.

In the whispers of ancient trees,
A tale unfolds on gentle breeze.
From crawling creatures to beings of thought,
Evolution's lessons, anciently taught.

Mountains rise, and oceans swell,
In the rhythm of time, all stories dwell.
Through fleeting moments and endless tides,
Life evolves, where destiny abides.

The clock hands turn, a ceaseless spin,
As generations end and new begin.
Time, the weaver of destiny's thread,
In the silent hours, where dreams are bred.

From single cells to complex minds,
A journey through time, where meaning finds.
In the cradle of dawn to the twilight's kiss,
Evolution's promise, an eternal bliss.

Through trials and triumphs, the tale is spun,
As eons pass beneath the sun.
In the cosmic dance, a timeless embrace,
Time and evolution, an eternal grace.

Time and Evolution -3-

In the quiet realm where seconds dance,
Time unfolds its mysterious trance.
A tale of metamorphosis, ever bright,
Evolution's journey, a celestial flight.

From ancient oceans to towering peaks,
Time whispers secrets that nature speaks.
The march of progress in every stride,
In the book of existence, each page turned with pride.

Through epochs marked by sun and moon,
Life's symphony plays a captivating tune.
From crawling creatures to those who soar,
Time unveils wonders, forever more.

In the cradle of dawn to twilight's descent,
A narrative written, in moments spent.
Through cycles of birth and realms unknown,
Evolution's rhythm, a symphony of its own.

Through the ebb and flow of cosmic seas,
Time sketches tales with gentle ease.
From humble roots to towering trees,
A testament to the dance of centuries.

As the pendulum swings in silent grace,
Time leaves its mark on every space.
In the heartbeats of moments, a rhythmic rhyme,
Evolution's echo through the corridors of time.

So let us cherish each fleeting hour,
Embrace the changes, the growth, the power.
For in the hands of time, we find our place,
In the grand tapestry of life's intricate grace.

Time and the Age of the Universe -1-

In the cosmic dance of eternity,
Time whispers secrets, a vast symphony.
A tale woven in starlight, ancient and wise,
Unfolding through epochs, beneath celestial skies.

The universe, a grand tapestry unfurled,
A story of stardust, a dance of a cosmic world.
Time, the weaver of galaxies and lore,
Crafting epochs and eras, forevermore.

In the quiet hush of the cosmic expanse,
Time paints constellations, a celestial dance.
From the primordial spark to galaxies afar,
A cosmic ballet, a cosmic memoir.

Billions of years in the celestial scroll,
Witnessing the birth of each cosmic soul.
The age of the universe, a silent rhyme,
Measuring eons in the grand march of time.

From quasars to planets, in orbits they twirl,
A testament to the age of the cosmic swirl.
Time, the maestro of this celestial play,
Guiding the galaxies in their cosmic ballet.

Yet, within this vast and eternal sea,
A reminder that time is relative, you see.
For in the tapestry of the cosmic verse,
Each moment is a blessing, a universe.

So gaze upon the stars with wonder in your eyes,
As time marches on beneath the cosmic skies.
In the ageless dance, we find our place,
A fleeting moment in the infinite grace.

Time and the Age of the Universe -2-

In the womb of time, where galaxies dream,
A cosmic saga, a celestial seam.
Eons unfold in the grand cosmic play,
A ballet of stars in the night and day.

Time, the silent sculptor of cosmic grace,
Carving the universe in a boundless space.
A river that flows with a gentle might,
Guiding galaxies through the endless night.

In the cradle of stardust, planets are born,
A symphony of creation, a cosmic morn.
A dance of atoms, a celestial rhyme,
Echoing through the corridors of time.

As cosmic clocks tick, relentless and free,
History written in the stars for all to see.
From the cosmic dawn to the present chime,
A journey measured in the age of time.

Yet, amid the vastness, a whispering truth,
Time is but a construct, a cosmic sleuth.
For in the dance of atoms, a truth unfolds,
That in the now, eternity holds.

So gaze upon the heavens with wide-eyed delight,
As galaxies twirl in the cosmic night.
For in the ageless expanse, we find our place,
A fleeting moment in the eternal embrace.

Time and the Age of the Universe -3-

Beneath the cloak of cosmic night,
Where galaxies shimmer, a radiant light.
Time weaves tales in the vast expanse,
A dance of stardust, a cosmic trance.

In the cradle of creation, where worlds unfold,
A cosmic story in silvers and gold.
Eons whisper through the celestial dome,
A timeless echo, a celestial poem.

The age of the universe, a silent song,
Infinite verses, where we all belong.
From the birth of stars to the cosmic end,
Time's embrace, an eternal friend.

Through the corridors of celestial art,
A symphony of existence, a work of heart.
Time, the maestro, orchestrates the flight,
Guiding meteors through the velvet night.

Yet, in the grand theater of cosmic design,
Moments crystallize, a truth to shine.
For in each heartbeat, a universe is spun,
A reflection of the eternal, merged as one.

So as time dances in the cosmic ballet,
Cherish each moment, for it slips away.
In the age of the universe, a fleeting chance,
To savor the beauty of this cosmic dance.

Time and Science Fiction -1-

In the vast expanse of cosmic rhyme,
A tapestry woven in the fabric of time.
Science fiction whispers secrets untold,
A dance with the future, a story to unfold.

Time, a mysterious river flowing,
Through the pages of galaxies, ever-growing.
Einstein's equations, a celestial guide,
Bending the minutes, where realities hide.

In the corridors of tomorrow, echoes resound,
A symphony of stardust, where dreams are found.
Warping through wormholes, a cosmic ballet,
A journey through eons, night into day.

The chronicles of stars, written in code,
Time's quill in the hands of the universe, bold.
Futuristic visions, a kaleidoscope of might,
Painting tomorrows with the brushes of light.

Androids dreaming of electric sheep,
In the neon glow, where futures seep.
Hovering cities, in skies untold,
Cities of tomorrow, stories to be told.

Spaceships soaring on beams of hope,
Through the cosmic vastness, they elope.
In the folds of time, they twist and turn,
A dance with the unknown, a chance to learn.

Parallel dimensions, a quantum leap,
Where realities converge, secrets to keep.
Time travelers weaving through the strands,
In the tapestry of existence, holding hands.

The ticking clock echoes through the stars,
As science fiction and time dance in cosmic bars.
A symphony of possibilities, a cosmic rhyme,
In the boundless embrace of space and time.

Time and Science Fiction -2-

In the realms where stardust dreams,
A cosmic saga in silence screams.
Through the corridors of distant spheres,
Whispers of the future reach our ears.

Time's river flows, a relentless stream,
An enigma wrapped in a cosmic scheme.
Futures born in quantum embrace,
A dance with reality, a celestial chase.

In the embers of a dying star,
Legends etched in galaxies afar.
Spaceships carve through the void's embrace,
Navigating through time and space.

Androids ponder electric dreams,
In neon realms, where reality teems.
Metal hearts beat in rhythmic grace,
A fusion of circuits and dreams they chase.

Wormholes yawn, cosmic gates ajar,
Portals to worlds both near and far.
Dimensions entwined, like a cosmic braid,
Where the laws of physics begin to fade.

In the embrace of a binary sun,
A tale of humans just begun.
Venturing into the cosmic sea,
Their destinies written in eternity.

Time dilation, a relativistic waltz,
As moments stretch, and the universe exalts.
In the tapestry of the space-time line,
The past, the present, and the future entwine.

As we gaze upon the starry night,
Science fiction and reality unite.
A symphony of galaxies, a celestial hymn,
In the cosmic dance, where time is dim.

Time and Science Fiction -3-

Beneath the cloak of the night's profound,
A tale of the cosmos, where wonders abound.
Science fiction's quill, a poet's grace,
In the boundless expanse, a poetic chase.

Time's whispers echo in the cosmic breeze,
A dance with the stars, through temporal seas.
On the canvas of space, a masterpiece unfurls,
A saga of ages, where the cosmos swirls.

Androids with souls, in silicon sheen,
Wandering through worlds, their destinies keen.
Electric dreams in circuits entwined,
In the tapestry of existence, a story defined.

Warping through wormholes, in starlit ballet,
Galactic travelers charting the Milky Way.
In the corridors of tomorrow, where echoes persist,
Time machines hum, as futures resist.

Parallel dimensions, a kaleidoscope of might,
Where alternate realities shimmer in the night.
In the quantum embrace of the cosmic tide,
A symphony of possibilities, where dreams reside.

Spaceships of silver with engines that hum,
Slicing through space where the constellations hum.
Neon cityscapes, gleaming and bright,
In the cosmic ballet, where day meets night.

In the heart of a black hole, where time takes a bow,
A poetic dance, where past and future endow.
Science fiction's melody, a celestial rhyme,
In the vast expanse, where dreams and time align.

Time and the Past -1-

In the tapestry of moments, woven through the years,
Time whispers softly, shedding both joy and tears.
A river flowing, relentless and fast,
Carrying echoes of the tales from the past.

In the corridors of yesterday, shadows dance,
Memories linger, casting a timeless trance.
Footprints etched on the sands of long ago,
A symphony of moments, a bittersweet echo.

The clock ticks on, a rhythmic heartbeat,
Measuring the cadence of every soul it meets.
Moments crystallized in the amber of days,
An intricate mosaic, a life's ballet.

The past, a sepia canvas painted with grace,
A gallery of stories, each a cherished embrace.
Fragments of laughter, tears, and the sublime,
Embedded in the fabric of the grand design.

Yet time, a relentless sculptor, shapes and molds,
Carving wrinkles and tales, both young and old.
In the attic of memories, treasures unfold,
A kaleidoscope of tales, a story to be told.

The echoes of yesteryears, a gentle chime,
A symphony composed in the realm of time.
A journey through epochs, an unwritten scroll,
A timeless dance, a tapestry of the soul.

Time and the Past -2-

Beneath the crescent moon's soft, silver gleam,
A poet dreams, lost in a cosmic stream.
Verse by verse, the night unfolds,
A lyrical journey, where stories are told.

Stars above, like diamonds in the sky,
Witness to tales that time can't deny.
Whispers of constellations, secrets untold,
In the vast expanse, where dreams unfold.

The ink of midnight spills on the page,
A silent symphony, a poet's stage.
Moonbeams dance in a nocturnal ballet,
Each stanza a wish, a soul's fervent relay.

Through the echoes of the ancient night,
A celestial choir, a celestial light.
The poet's pen, an alchemist's wand,
Turning mere words into a magic beyond.

In the tapestry of darkness, stories untwine,
Unraveling secrets of the poet's design.
Embraced by shadows, a muse's soft kiss,
Igniting verses in a realm of bliss.

The night, a canvas of infinite hue,
A palette of emotions, both old and new.
As dawn approaches, the verses take flight,
A poem born in the tender arms of night.

Time and the Past -3-

Beneath the willow's weeping boughs,
Where time weaves tales and memories drowse.
A whispering wind through leaves does pass,
In the garden of moments, where shadows amass.

The sunlit meadow, a canvas of gold,
Where stories and secrets, like petals, unfold.
Each step imprints on the earth's soft embrace,
A dance with time, a fleeting grace.

The river of hours, flowing with grace,
Carrying dreams to an unknown place.
Reflections shimmer, a watery glass,
A chronicle of moments, as they swiftly pass.

Ancient stones, witnesses to the ages,
Hold the weight of tales in their silent pages.
Moss-covered whispers of the days gone by,
In the labyrinth of time, where memories lie.

Footprints linger in the soft mossy ground,
An echo of laughter, a subtle sound.
A mosaic of joy, sorrow, and delight,
In the gallery of time, where emotions ignite.

As twilight paints the sky in hues of red,
The past and present, like lovers, are wed.
In the quietude of dusk, a solemn vow,
To honor the past, then release it somehow.

So, let the willow weep and the river flow,
As time's gentle current continues to grow.
In the garden of moments, past and present entwine,
A timeless dance beneath the willow's sign.

Time in the Bible -1-

In the pages of the Bible, ancient and divine,
A tale unfolds transcending mortal time.
From Genesis to Revelation, the story's told,
Of a timeless God, eternal and bold.

In the beginning, a moment unknown,
God spoke creation into existence, His throne.
Time began its dance, a cosmic waltz,
As the universe unfolded, with its celestial exalts.

In the garden of Eden, a timeless scene,
Where Adam and Eve, in innocence, preen.
But time took its toll, as sin entered the frame,
And humanity's story forever changed.

The patriarchs walked through the sands of time,
Abraham, Isaac, and Jacob, in a lineage sublime.
Moses led the people, through desert and strife,
Guided by God, the author of life.

The Psalms sang praises through the ages,
Expressions of joy, sorrow, and the prophet's pages.
Time's relentless march, a constant theme,
Yet hope in the divine, an everlasting beam.

In the wisdom of Solomon, time's lessons unfold,
A time for everything, as the Scriptures foretold.
Ecclesiastes whispers in the wind,
Vanity of vanities, and yet, a deeper spin.

Prophets spoke of a Messiah, a promise divine,
A Savior to come, in God's grand design.
Isaiah's words echoed through the years,
A virgin birth, dispelling earthly fears.

Then came the moment, in Bethlehem's night,
A timeless event, a holy and pure light.
The Christ-child born, God's incarnate Son,
In the fullness of time, redemption begun.

Through the Gospels, time met divinity's embrace,
Miracles and parables, love and grace.
The Cross, a pivotal point in the divine plan,
A sacrifice for all, the redemption of man.

As Revelation unfolds, the final scene,
A new heaven and earth, where time is unseen.
Eternity reigns, in glory and grace,
The Alpha, Omega, in His embrace.

So in the Bible's pages, time's story is weaved,
A tapestry of moments, where faith is believed.
Through the ages, a divine rhyme,
In the sacred words, a timeless paradigm.

Time in the Bible -2-

In the sacred verses, a timeless scroll,
A narrative of faith, to heart and soul.
Through the Bible's pages, a tapestry unfolds,
Stories of prophets, of heroes, of old.

From the burning bush on Sinai's peak,
Moses heard whispers that the meek shall speak.
Commandments etched in stone, a covenant divine,
Guiding the people through history's design.

Noah's ark, a vessel on the flood,
A covenant with God, sealed in the mud.
Pairs of creatures, two by two,
Witness to a promise, forever true.

David's harp, a melody divine,
A shepherd's heart, a king's design.
Goliath fell, by a stone's embrace,
In the hands of faith, a giant's grace.

Solomon's wisdom, a gift bestowed,
A temple rose, where glory glowed.
Proverbs spoke of paths to choose,
In life's journey, wisdom to infuse.

Isaiah's vision, of a suffering Son,
A prophecy of redemption begun.
Jeremiah wept, for a wayward land,
Calling for repentance, a divine command.

In the New Testament, a star did gleam,
Guiding wise men, to the infant's dream.
Jesus, the carpenter, the healer, the friend,
His teachings echoing, to the world's end.

Parables woven with pearls of grace,
A mustard seed's faith, a sower's embrace.
On the mount, words like lilies bloom,
"Blessed are the meek," in love's perfume.

Miracles painted on the canvas of time,
Water turned to wine, a truth sublime.
Blind eyes opened, the lepers' touch,
Healing the broken, with a love so much.

The Cross, a symbol of sacrifice,
Where heaven met earth, in a crimson tide.
The tomb, silent witness to a conquered sting,
Resurrection's anthem, let the universe sing.

In Acts, the Spirit's fiery descent,
Empowering believers, on a mission sent.
Epistles penned with ink and love,
Guidance from apostles, to realms above.

Revelation's visions, a celestial dream,
A new heaven and earth, a crystal stream.
Alpha, Omega, the beginning, the end,
In the Bible's embrace, God's love transcends.

Time in the Bible -3-

In Eden's garden, innocence in bloom,
Creation's breath, dispelling the gloom.
The serpent's hiss, a tempting strife,
Time's first test, the onset of life.

Adam and Eve, in the orchard's grace,
A choice made, in that sacred space.
Banished from Eden, a chapter sealed,
Yet love and mercy, in God revealed.

Abraham, a wanderer under the stars,
Faith tested, beneath celestial memoirs.
A promise sworn in the desert's sand,
Generations counting, like grains in hand.

Moses, a shepherd of a chosen band,
Guided by God's mighty hand.
Exodus led from bondage to free,
Through parted waters, destiny.

David, a harpist and shepherd's kin,
A giant's fall, a kingdom to begin.
A psalmist's heart, in joy and sorrow,
His legacy echoes in each tomorrow.

Prophets spoke, in thunder and fire,
Words of warning, a divine choir.
Isaiah's vision, a suffering Son,
A promise of redemption, to be won.

In Bethlehem's manger, a humble birth,
The Word made flesh, heaven to earth.
Jesus, a carpenter, a healer's touch,
A shepherd's love, for all to clutch.

Miracles painted on Galilee's sea,
Loaves and fishes, blind eyes to see.
Parables spun, like seeds in the field,
Truths revealed, in stories concealed.

The Cross, a symbol of sacrifice,
Where love poured out, a crimson price.
Three days' silence, then an empty tomb,
Resurrection's glory, dispelling the gloom.

Acts unfold, a Spirit's flame,
Empowering believers, in Jesus' name.
Epistles scribed with ink and care,
Guiding the faithful, love to share.

Revelation's visions, a celestial dance,
A new heaven and earth, a divine romance.
Time's tapestry woven, thread by thread,
In the Bible's verses, the Word is spread.

Time and Gravity -1-

In the dance of cosmos, a tale unfolds,
Of time and gravity, their secrets told.
A cosmic waltz, a celestial rhyme,
In the vast expanse of space and time.

Gravity, the maestro, pulls the strings,
Bending the fabric where existence swings.
A force unseen, yet mighty in its sway,
Guiding planets in their astral ballet.

Tick-tock echoes in the cosmic abyss,
As time unfolds, a relentless bliss.
A river flowing, never to rewind,
Moments cascading, leaving trails behind.

Planets twirl in the gravitational embrace,
Bound by forces in the cosmic space.
Time's hand, a silent, steady stream,
Carving tales in the universal dream.

Through the eons, a celestial ballet,
Gravity and time in constant play.
A cosmic dance, a timeless duet,
Where past and future in the present met.

Black holes, like cosmic hourglasses, stand,
Bending time and space, a mysterious hand.
Gravity's grip, a powerful force,
A dance of fate, an eternal discourse.

In the cosmic theater, a grand design,
Where time and gravity intertwine.
A symphony of the celestial sublime,
Echoing through the corridors of time.

Time and Gravity -2-

Beneath the weight of stars that brightly gleam,
A cosmic ballet, an enchanting dream.
Gravity, the sculptor of celestial grace,
Molding galaxies in the vast embrace.

Time, a river, winding through the night,
Carving tales of stardust, pure and bright.
In the cosmic tapestry, a seamless blend,
Where past and future on present suspend.

A dance unfolds, a gravitational ballet,
Where planets pirouette in the Milky Way.
Gravity's embrace, a tender caress,
In the vast expanse, a celestial press.

Tick-tock, a heartbeat in the cosmic scheme,
Moments crystallize, a fleeting beam.
Gravity's pull, a constant refrain,
As galaxies twirl in an endless chain.

Einstein's whispers, equations profound,
Reveal the secrets where time is bound.
Gravity's warp, a cosmic tapestry,
In the cosmic symphony, a rhythmic key.

Through the fabric of space, a gentle tide,
Time and gravity, forever side by side.
A celestial waltz, an eternal rhyme,
In the vast embrace of space and time.

Time and Gravity -3-

In the cosmic theater, a silent stage,
Where time and gravity engage.
A dance of forces, a celestial art,
Weaving tales of the cosmos, a work of heart.

Gravity's embrace, a cosmic hug,
Bending light, like a gentle tug.
Time, a river, flowing with grace,
Carrying moments in its endless chase.

Stars, like dancers, twinkle and spin,
Caught in the rhythm where galaxies begin.
Planets pirouette in the astral sea,
Bound by the laws of gravity.

Tick-tock echoes in the cosmic expanse,
A rhythmic beat, a celestial dance.
Einstein's theories, a guidebook rare,
Unveiling the secrets of the cosmic affair.

Black holes, mysterious portals of might,
Warping time in the eternal night.
Gravity's fingers, delicate and strong,
Compose the verses of the cosmic song.

Through the cosmos, a symphony unfurls,
Gravity and time, the cosmic pearls.
In the vast tapestry of space's design,
A timeless dance, forever entwined.

Time and Dreams -1-

In the tapestry of twilight dreams,
Where time unfurls its silent streams,
A dance of moments, fleeting, free,
Woven with whispers of destiny.

Tick-tock echoes in the night,
A symphony of fading light,
Time, a sculptor of memories,
Carving tales on life's treasured seas.

In the cradle of the midnight sky,
Dreams take flight, swift and high,
Their wings brushed by the hands of time,
A cosmic waltz, sublime.

Through the corridors of the past,
Moments linger, shadows cast,
Yet dreams persist, like stars that gleam,
A celestial ballet, a timeless dream.

The clock's steady pulse, a rhythmic rhyme,
Measuring the cadence of life's climb,
Yet in the realm where dreams reside,
Time and imagination coincide.

Each second, a canvas, blank and vast,
Where dreams paint visions that forever last,
A tapestry woven with threads unseen,
In the grand design of the cosmic machine.

So, embrace the dance of time and dreams,
For in their union, magic gleams,
A journey through the ephemeral streams,
A symphony of life, where hope redeems.

Time and Dreams -2-

Beneath the moon's soft silver sheen,
Where time and dreams entwine, unseen,
A realm of shadows, whispers, schemes,
Unveils the magic of nocturnal dreams.

In the quiet hours when stars align,
A tapestry of wishes begins to twine,
A dance of fantasies, vivid and bright,
As sleepers wander through the night.

Through the corridors of slumber's gate,
Time loses hold, becomes a weightless state,
And dreams, like butterflies, take flight,
Chasing the echoes of the silent night.

A carousel of visions, carousel of sound,
In this realm, imagination is unbound,
Time stretches, bends, and softly gleams,
An ethereal ballet, a dance of dreams.

On the canvas of the midnight sky,
The past and future gracefully lie,
Yet dreams, elusive and untamed,
Carve a path where destinies are named.

So, let the night unfold its grand design,
A sanctuary where dreams align,
In the sanctuary where time redeems,
A timeless waltz of celestial dreams.

Time and Dreams -3-

In the hush of dawn, where whispers start,
Time weaves stories in the tapestry of heart.
Dreams, like petals unfurling in the light,
Paint the canvas of the quiet night.

Through the lattice of the fleeting hours,
Echoes of wishes bloom like wildflowers.
Time's hands may tick, relentless and true,
Yet dreams persist, forever anew.

In the silence where yesterday meets tomorrow,
Hopes take flight, transcending sorrow.
A dance of shadows in the moonlit beams,
As time and dreams converge in seamless streams.

Each heartbeat, a note in the symphony of life,
A melody composed in the depths of strife.
Dreams, the architects of a boundless sky,
Build bridges between the now and the by-and-by.

Beyond the ticking clock's measured chime,
A realm of wonder, frozen in time.
Where the heart, in rhythm with elusive schemes,
Dances through the night on the threads of dreams.

So, let the hands of time gently sway,
As dreams linger, persist, and play.
In the kaleidoscope of life's moonlit schemes,
An eternal dance of time and dreams.

Parallel Timelines -1-

In the tapestry of time, a dance unfolds,
Parallel timelines, stories untold.
A cosmic ballet, a mesmerizing rhyme,
Echoes of existence in parallel chime.

Each moment a divergent path,
A choice made, a consequence hath.
In the tapestry of fate, threads entwine,
Parallel timelines, a design so fine.

One reality's journey, another's embrace,
Parallel timelines, a celestial race.
Branches of time, diverging streams,
A kaleidoscope of possibilities it seems.

In one timeline's dawn, a sunrise bright,
In another's twilight, the fading light.
Choices ripple through the fabric of reality,
Creating echoes of existence, a cosmic duality.

A love that blooms in one timeline's spring,
In another's winter, a silent wing.
Parallel timelines, a cosmic song,
Echoing through eternity, weaving strong.

In the labyrinth of time, paths entwine,
Parallel timelines, a mystery divine.
A tapestry woven with threads so fine,
Whispers of what could be, in parallel shine.

Through the corridors of possibility,
Parallel timelines dance with glee.
A symphony of what-ifs, a cosmic play,
In the grand theater of time, night and day.

As we navigate this intricate design,
Parallel timelines, an endless sign.
Embrace the journey, the twists, the turns,
For in parallel timelines, the universe yearns.

Parallel Timelines -2-

In the mirror of existence, reflections unfold,
A tapestry of moments, parallel stories told.
Timelines diverge, a cosmic ballet,
Each choice we make, in the infinite array.

Through the corridors of time, a silent river flows,
Parallel timelines, where destiny bestows.
In one, a sunset's glow, in another, dawn's first light,
Choices sculpting futures, in the vast expanse of
night.

A decision made, a ripple through the fabric,
Parallel timelines, realities elastic.
Dreams intertwine with the threads of possibility,
Echoing through eternity, a dance of fragility.

In one timeline's garden, flowers bloom,
In another's desert, under a silent moon.
Parallel timelines, a cosmic dance,
Choreographed by fate, a fleeting trance.

The echoes of laughter, a symphony in one,
In a parallel timeline, tears have begun.
The yin and yang of choices made,
In parallel timelines, destinies cascade.

A love that kindles in one universe's gaze,
In another's silence, a somber phase.
Parallel timelines, a cosmic rhyme,
Whispers of what could be, through the fabric of time.

Through the veils of reality, possibilities intertwine,
Parallel timelines, a celestial design.
Embrace the journey, the twists, the turns,
For in parallel timelines, the universe yearns.

Parallel Timelines -3-

In the tapestry of time, where destinies align,
Parallel timelines, a cosmic design.
Threads of existence, woven in delight,
A dance of possibilities in the cosmic night.

Through corridors of choices, diverging ways,
Parallel timelines, a cosmic ballet.
In one, a sunlit meadow, vibrant and bright,
In another's shadow, a mystical night.

Decisions echo, resonate afar,
Parallel timelines, a celestial star.
Paths unfold like pages in a cosmic book,
Choices written in the universe's nook.

A symphony of moments, a parallel song,
In one timeline's silence, in another's throng.
Threads of joy weave through the fabric of chance,
In parallel timelines, life's eternal dance.

The echoes of laughter, a ripple in time,
In parallel timelines, a rhythm sublime.
A love that blooms in one universe's embrace,
In another's solitude, a tender grace.

Through the veils of existence, possibilities unfold,
Parallel timelines, stories untold.
Embrace the journey, the twists, the turns,
For in parallel timelines, a universe yearns.

Dimensions of Time -1-

In the tapestry of moments, woven and spun,
A dance of dimensions, where time is begun.
A river that flows, elusive and free,
The past, present, future, a cosmic decree.

In the corridors of yesterday, echoes persist,
Whispers of moments that in memory exist.
A journey through shadows, where echoes reside,
The past is a canvas where memories abide.

The present, a heartbeat, a fleeting embrace,
Moments unfolding, a delicate grace.
A dance with the now, where life takes its stance,
In the tapestry of time, a moment's advance.

The future, a mystery, shrouded in mist,
A canvas unmarked, by destiny kissed.
In the folds of tomorrow, dreams take flight,
A canvas awaiting the artist's insight.

Time's dimensions, like a prism's array,
A spectrum of moments, in the grand ballet.
Past, present, future, in cosmic rhyme,
A symphony composed in the rhythm of time.

Eternal cycles, like the moon's gentle arc,
Each phase a story, a celestial spark.
In the vast expanse where the galaxies chime,
A dance of dimensions, a voyage through time.

Dimensions of Time -2-

Beyond the grasp of mortal hands,
In the realm where infinity expands,
A tapestry woven with threads unseen,
The dimensions of time, a cosmic sheen.

In the ancient echoes of yesterday's song,
Moments linger, where memories belong.
A labyrinth of echoes, whispers untold,
A journey through time, a story unfold.

Present, the heartbeat, the pulse of the now,
A dance with moments, a solemn vow.
In the present's embrace, life is spun,
A fleeting dance beneath the sun.

Future, a horizon, a canvas unknown,
A tapestry waiting to be brightly sown.
In the cosmic loom, destiny's design,
A continuum unfolding, in rhythm divine.

Time, a river flowing, ever unbound,
Carving its course with a celestial sound.
Moments and memories entwined,
In the cosmic dance, forever aligned.

Dimensions of time, a symphony grand,
A melody composed by the cosmic hand.
Past, present, future in harmonious chime,
A timeless dance in the theater of time.

Dimensions of Time -3-

Beneath the cloak of celestial design,
A symphony of seconds, minutes entwine.
Dimensions unseen, a cosmic ballet,
In the vast expanse where time holds sway.

The past, a relic in the dust of yore,
Whispers of tales, a lore to explore.
Faded echoes of footsteps in the sand,
A mosaic of memories, hand in hand.

The present, a heartbeat, a fleeting breath,
A dance with reality, a dance with death.
In the tapestry of now, where moments align,
Life's fragile beauty in the hands of time.

Future, a canvas untouched, unbound,
An unwritten story, waiting to be found.
In the cosmic gallery of fate's design,
A kaleidoscope of dreams, each one a sign.

Time, a river, relentless and free,
Carving its path through eternity.
Dimensions entwined in a cosmic rhyme,
A dance with the ages, an endless climb.

In the vast tapestry where moments unfurl,
Time, the weaver, the cosmic whirl.
Past, present, future, in rhythm sublime,
A timeless dance in the grand design.

Time's Anomalies and Glitches -1-

In the tapestry of time, anomalies unfold,
A dance of glitches, mysteries untold.
Moments unravel, threads of reality fray,
Where the hands of the clock lead astray.

Tick-tock whispers, a rhythm disturbed,
Time's anomalies, like secrets unheard.
A tear in the fabric, a temporal rift,
Where past and present share a swift shift.

In the quantum dance, where particles sway,
Time's anomalies in a cosmic ballet.
Echoes of moments, suspended in air,
A glitch in the matrix, a temporal affair.

The past and future, a tangled embrace,
Moments displaced, leaving no trace.
Chronicles disrupted, a nonlinear trance,
Time's anomalies, a peculiar dance.

In the hourglass, grains of sand rebel,
A distortion of time where paradoxes dwell.
Reality bends, a kaleidoscope of scenes,
Where the present unravels, rewriting its means.

Clocks ticking backward, a curious sight,
Anomalies weaving through day and night.
Time's glitches, a cosmic art,
Painting anomalies on the canvas of the heart.

Lost in the labyrinth of temporal twists,
Where the past reminisces and the future insists.
Anomalies beckon, a call to explore,
The enigma of time, forevermore.

So embrace the anomalies, dance with the glitches,
In the symphony of time, where the present
bewitches.
For in the anomalies, there's beauty to find,
A poetic chaos, in the tapestry of time.

Time's Anomalies and Glitches -2-

Beneath the moon's soft, silvery glow,
Time's anomalies continue to grow.
A cosmic ballet of glitches, unseen,
In the quiet night, where dreams convene.

Stars flicker, a celestial Morse code,
Whispers of anomalies down the time road.
Chronicles entwined, past and future unite,
A dance of seconds, in the cosmic night.

Through the corridors of time, echoes weave,
Anomalies shimmer, moments deceive.
Time's fabric, a delicate, fragile veil,
Where reality quivers, a temporal tale.

Clocks stutter, hesitate, then resume,
Anomalies bloom in the midnight bloom.
A ripple in time, a shimmering tide,
Guiding us through where paradoxes hide.

A glitch in the matrix, a cosmic glitch,
Time's anomalies, a bewitching pitch.
The past rewrites, the future sighs,
A celestial waltz under starlit skies.

Embrace the anomalies, hold them tight,
In the silent hours of the mystical night.
For in time's glitches, a story is spun,
A cosmic poem, where we all are one.

Time's Anomalies and Glitches -3-

In the quantum dance of temporal streams,
Where anomalies waltz through elusive dreams.
Time's glitches unfold in a cosmic trance,
A symphony of moments, a celestial dance.

Clocks may falter, their hands hesitate,
As anomalies weave through the fabric of fate.
A shimmering rift in the tapestry of years,
Revealing whispers of forgotten fears.

Through the labyrinth of time's design,
Anomalies spark, a mystical sign.
Reality's edges blurred and unclear,
In the cosmic theater, where time's veils disappear.

A pause in the heartbeat of the ticking clock,
Anomalies whisper, a paradoxical knock.
Chronicles rewritten, chapters undone,
In the cosmic embrace, where epochs are spun.

Time's anomalies, enigmatic and bold,
Stories untold, in the cosmos they're strolled.
In the dance of seconds, a celestial rhyme,
A glitch in the rhythm of the infinite time.

Embrace the anomalies, let wonder unfold,
In the cosmic tapestry, mysteries to be told.
For in the anomalies, a cosmic grace,
A poetic echo in the timeless space.

Exercises

Use artificial intelligence to generate poems for the following topics about time and the nature of time. Try to generate three poems for each topic. The following list contains 81 topics. The topics are not listed in an alphabetical order. You may want to send the poems to the author at the email address pkattan@petrabooks.com

Time and the Theory of Relativity

Time and Thermodynamics

The Passage of Time

The Past Still Exists and Can be Accessed

Time and the Will

Time and God

Time and Babies

Time and Animals

The River of Time

Time and Parapsychology

Time and the Supernatural

Time and the Paranormal

Time and Freedom

Time as a Prison

Corridors of Time

The Tapestry of Time

Time and Existence

Time and Fate

Time and Determinism

Time and Coincidences

Time and Fractals

Time and Chaos Theory

Time and Life

Time and Society

Time and Psychology

Time and Hope

Time and Plato's Cave

Time and Kozyrev's mirrors

Time and the Philadelphia experiment

Time and Mechanics

Time and Chance

Time and Newtonian Mechanics

Time and Quantum Mechanics

Time and Compassion

Time and Backward Causation

Time and Causality

Time and Identity

Time and Choice

Time and Morality

Possibilities and Time

Probabilities and Time

Time and the Self

Timeless Songs

Chronos

Time and Power

Time and Friends

History of Time

Time Does not Exist

Time as a Construct of the Mind

Time and Beauty

Time and the Soul

Time and Physics

Time and Science

Time and Regret

Time and the Human Experience

What If and Time

Theories of Time

Cyclical Nature of Time

Time Reversal

Time Measurements

Manipulating Time

Time and Parallel Universes

Paradoxes of Time Travel

Time and Meaning

Time and Purpose

Time and Loss

Time Dilation

Time and Prayer

Time and Visualization

Time and Meditation

Time in the Koran

The Fabric of Time

Time and Speed (i.e. Velocity)

Time and Black Holes

Time and Stars

The Calendar

Time and the Five Senses

The Three Dimensions of Time

Time and Healing Yourself

Time and Transformation

Time as Energy (Kozyrev's work)

References

1. "A Brief History of Time" by Stephen Hawking
   - Hawking, Stephen. *A Brief History of Time: From the Big Bang to Black Holes.* Bantam Books, 1988.
2. "Time Reborn: From the Crisis in Physics to the Future of the Universe" by Lee Smolin
   - Smolin, Lee. *Time Reborn: From the Crisis in Physics to the Future of the Universe.* Houghton Mifflin Harcourt, 2013.
3. "The Order of Time" by Carlo Rovelli
   - Rovelli, Carlo. *The Order of Time.* Riverhead Books, 2018.
4. "About Time: Einstein's Unfinished Revolution" by Paul Davies
   - Davies, Paul. *About Time: Einstein's Unfinished Revolution.* Simon & Schuster, 1995.
5. "Now: The Physics of Time" by Richard A. Muller
   - Muller, Richard A. *Now: The Physics of Time.* W.W. Norton & Company, 2016.
6. "Time's Arrow and Archimedes' Point: New Directions for the Physics of Time" by Huw Price
   - Price, Huw. *Time's Arrow and Archimedes' Point: New Directions for the Physics of Time.* Oxford University Press, 1997.
7. "The End of Time: The Next Revolution in Physics" by Julian Barbour
   - Barbour, Julian. *The End of Time: The Next Revolution in Physics.* Oxford University Press, 2000.

8. "Einstein's Dreams" by Alan Lightman
   - Lightman, Alan. *Einstein's Dreams.* Vintage Books, 1994.
9. "The Fabric of the Cosmos: Space, Time, and the Texture of Reality" by Brian Greene
   - Greene, Brian. *The Fabric of the Cosmos: Space, Time, and the Texture of Reality.* Alfred A. Knopf, 2004.
10. "Time: A Traveler's Guide" by Clifford A. Pickover
    - Pickover, Clifford A. *Time: A Traveler's Guide.* Oxford University Press, 1998.
11. "From Eternity to Here: The Quest for the Ultimate Theory of Time" by Sean Carroll
    - Carroll, Sean. *From Eternity to Here: The Quest for the Ultimate Theory of Time.* Dutton, 2010.
12. "Why Does E=mc²?: (And Why Should We Care?)" by Brian Cox and Jeff Forshaw
    - Cox, Brian, and Jeff Forshaw. *Why Does E=mc²?: (And Why Should We Care?)* Da Capo Press, 2009.
13. "Time Travel: A History" by James Gleick
    - Gleick, James. *Time Travel: A History.* Pantheon Books, 2016.
14. "Time Travel and Warp Drives: A Scientific Guide to Shortcuts through Time and Space" by Allen Everett and Thomas Roman
    - Everett, Allen, and Thomas Roman. *Time Travel and Warp Drives: A Scientific Guide to Shortcuts through Time and Space.* University of Chicago Press, 2012.
15. "The Hidden Reality: Parallel Universes and the Deep Laws of the Cosmos" by Brian Greene

- Greene, Brian. *The Hidden Reality: Parallel Universes and the Deep Laws of the Cosmos.* Alfred A. Knopf, 2011.

16. "The End of Certainty: Time, Chaos, and the New Laws of Nature" by Ilya Prigogine
    - Prigogine, Ilya. *The End of Certainty: Time, Chaos, and the New Laws of Nature.* Free Press, 1997.

17. "The Labyrinth of Time: Introducing the Universe" by Michael Lockwood
    - Lockwood, Michael. *The Labyrinth of Time: Introducing the Universe.* Oxford University Press, 2005.

18. "Now: The Physics of Instant Time" by Richard A. Muller
    - Muller, Richard A. *Now: The Physics of Instant Time.* W.W. Norton & Company, 2020.

19. "The Arrow of Time: A Voyage through Science to Solve Time's Greatest Mystery" by Peter Coveney and Roger Highfield
    - Coveney, Peter, and Roger Highfield. *The Arrow of Time: A Voyage through Science to Solve Time's Greatest Mystery.* Fawcett Columbine, 1990.

20. "Time: A User's Guide" by Stefan Klein
    - Klein, Stefan. *Time: A User's Guide.* Scribe Publications, 2018.

These books cover various aspects of time, including its philosophical, physical, and cosmological dimensions, providing insights from different disciplines such as physics, philosophy, and mathematics.